5 MUST KNOW >>>>>>
secrets
for today's
college girl

L A U R E N   P.  I E

Frederick Fell Publishers, Inc
2131 Hollywood Blvd., Suite 305
Hollywood, Fl 33020
www.Fellpub.com
email: Fellpub@aol.com

Frederick Fell Publishers, Inc
2131 Hollywood Blvd., Suite 305
Hollywood, Fl 33020

For information about special discounts for bulk purchases. Please contact Frederick Fell Special Sales at business@fellpublishers.com.

Designed by Elena Solis
Edited by Kimberly Coffey

Manufactured in the United States of America

14 13 12 11 10 9 8 7 6 5 4 3 2

Library of Congress Cataloging-in-Publication Data

Salamone, Lauren P., 1960-
  5 must-know secrets for today's college girl / Lauren P. Salamone.
    p. cm.
  Includes index.
  ISBN 978-0-88391-183-9 (pbk. : alk. paper)
1. Women college students--Life skills guides. I. Title. II. Title: Five must-know secrets for today's college girl.
  LC1756.S25 2011
  378.1'9808422--dc22

                            2011016241

ISBN 13: 978-0-88391-183-9

Praise for 5 Must-Know Secrets for Today's College Girl

"I know from my years of experience as a college adviser that young women entering college are fortunate, indeed, to have Lauren Salamone unlocking five secrets to ease their entry and lead them toward achieving their goals. They will benefit greatly from Lauren's warm and friendly voice, the situations she describes, and the strategies she proposes. Moreover, they will be encouraged by the many inspiring stories that previous students share. Readers who engage with 5 Must-Know Secrets will discover a clear sense of direction and gain a strong sense of confidence."

— Dr. Marilyn Sobelman, Associate Professor of Teaching and Learning
New York University

"These are secrets some women learn… eventually. But Lauren Salamone draws upon her years as a college-student mentor to reveal them to young women sooner rather than later with specific suggestions of insightful, obviously productive, rewarding actions to maximize each day of their college years. The difference? For her lucky readers – an enriched college experience…and life!"

— Julie Goodyear, Senior Admissions Officer
Educational Foundation Scholarship Program

"*College Women* – get ready to add a secret ingredient to your lives at school. You're going to be in the driver's seat every leg of your journey after reading this book. You'll not only figure out what you truly want, but you'll know exactly how to make it happen!"

— Geanine Thompson, President, MBAGoddess.com
MBA Admissions Consultant

"Students spend so much time and effort getting into college. It's about time they have an inspirational book to arm them for success once they get there! Not only does *5 Must-Know Secrets for Today's College Girl* answer this call, but it specifically reveals to college girls how to implement a simple and proven system to accelerate their success in college and for the rest of their lives."

— Jo-Anne Gretemeyer, Educational Counselor & Advisor
Plymouth North High School

"This book not only sets girls up for an abundantly successful college experience, but it puts them directly on the path to real-world success after graduation. Lauren speaks to college girls in an upbeat and energizing style, inspiring them to accomplish more in college than they ever dreamed they were capable of achieving."

— James Malinchak, Co-Author, *Chicken Soup for the College Soul*
Founder, www.BigMoneySpeaker.com
Two-Time "College Speaker of the Year"

"STOP! Don't leave for college without 5 Must-Know Secrets! And if you're already there – HURRY and pick up a copy! This book bridges the gap between a mediocre college experience and a home-run!"

— Ashley DePasquale
Lesley University '09

"Secrets No More! Why wasn't this book around when I was in college? It's fun to read, yet profound in message, offering college girls crucial insight that is at once eye-opening, empowering, and life-changing!"

— Julia Wyghe, Parent of two College Girls
Scituate, RI

"College can be stressful. But once students apply Lauren Salamone's *5 Must-Know Secrets*, they will navigate their journeys with ease and clarity, resulting in a much more rewarding college experience!"

— Shari Sutton, Associate Director of College Counseling
Choate Rosemary Hall

For Molly, Ashley, & Christina.

Your metamorphoses from inquisitive, pithy teens to
vibrant, accomplished young women inspire me beyond words.

Acknowledgments

What an inspiring and enlightening adventure the creation of this book has been. It's a project I've embraced with passion but not one I could have done alone. This book would not have been possible without the help and support of a team of individuals to whom I am deeply grateful.

To Paul, my eternally-supportive and loving husband, thanks for valuing my commitment to making this book a reality and for whipping up wondrous culinary delights when I disappeared from the kitchen for days at a time. You are an amazing inspiration to me. I simply couldn't have done it without you.

Thank you to my dear sisters – to Sandy for your invaluable feedback, editing, and brainstorming, as well as your zeal for this project from day-one; and to Suzy for your support and enthusiasm through each milestone. Such gifts you both are to me.

Thank you to the team at Frederick Fell for your skill in creating this book: Don Lessne, for your commitment to the success of this project from idea through book-completion; Kim Coffey, for your encouragement and expert editing; Elena Solis, for your top-shelf creative design every step of the way.

I'm tremendously appreciative of my friends and colleagues who provided feedback and support in so many ways through the multiple stages of this project: Donna, Mica, Diane, Jenny, Judy, Stacie, Jamie, Emma, Jerry, Marty, Ed, and David; Emily Desmery for your beautiful star-graphics; Donna Petrangelo for allowing me to test the waters of my book-format with your students; Chris Hamilton for your continued interest and feedback afterward; Sharon Lasky and Elizabeth Hughes for sharing your students with me, as well. Thank you all.

Nothing crystallizes a message more effectively than real-life examples. I'm so very grateful to this book's contributors – my own former students as well as newer additions to the team – for sharing your fascinating and diverse stories. Because of your generosity and candor, today's college women have the opportunity to benefit from your experiences. I value immensely your participation in this project.

Special thanks to all the students – past and present – who have chosen me as one of your mentors. You continue to inspire and encourage me and are so very kind to tell me I do the same for you. Without you, I would not have fully realized the significance of the message I share in this book. Without you, there would be no book.

And finally, thank you to my readers for valuing your own success enough to read this book. I wish each of you a rich and rewarding journey through college… and for the rest of your life.

Note from Lauren 11

Why I wrote this book

Part I
Discover the 5-Must Know Secrets

Introduction..15

The 5 Secrets to make you Shine in college!

Section One STRENGTH.......................................20

What makes YOU unique?

Section Two INSTINCT.......................................38

What does your ideal life look like?

Section Three MIND...58

Orchestrate your college experience with confidence!

Section Four SOUL..84

How do you stay upbeat and energized?

Section Five BODY...108

How do you get what you want out of college?

Time to Shine!...124

The greatest gift you can give yourself… and the world!

Part II

The 5 Must-Know Secrets Action Guide

Section One...132

STRENGTH in Action

Section Two..149

INSTINCT in Action

Section Three..154

MIND in Action

Section Four...162

SOUL in Action

Section Five...170

BODY in Action

Appendix A...184

Guide to Mindful Breathing

Appendix B...187

Access the Guided Inspiration

Index...188

About the Author..192

Note from Lauren

Why I wrote this book

Do you remember your favorite teacher? Mine was Mrs. Hellman, third grade. I'll never forget the day she wore one orange shoe and one purple shoe to school. We, of course, felt compelled to point out that one orange and one purple did not a pair make. But she disagreed. She told us she was quite sure it was a pair since she had another pair just like it at home. We got a real kick out of Mrs. Hellman. I can still picture the colorful dresses she wore and her red hair piled on top of her head. We came to school each day eager to learn what she had in store for us, and she never disappointed!

My desire to be a teacher began to surface way back in Mrs. Hellman's class. Sure enough, years later – after a career in the corporate world – I eventually followed that calling. My goal was to have my own special rapport with my students, one that would keep them eager to find out what I had cooked up to make learning fun…or at least interesting. To this day, I think I was probably one of few high school teachers who actually had her students singing in class on a regular basis. Some of them were probably ready to deck me, but they weren't bored.

I loved my years as a high school English teacher. My students inspired me, and I relished the opportunity to share with them my passion for language and literature. In many ways I learned as much from my students as they did from me, while together we explored the material-at-hand, as well as plenty of other compelling topics that arose along the way.

It was during those teaching years that I started my work as a college-student mentor. I found that many of my students were staying in touch with me after they graduated. In fact, quite a few of them reached out for advice when they moved on to college. As it was primarily the girls who stayed in touch, my experience – and much of what I share in this book – is based upon mentoring those female students. So, College Girls, it is TO YOU that I'm writing. (Of course, everyone is welcome to read on.)

When my own students began to reach out to me from their respective colleges and universities, I responded, eager to see them succeed. I tapped into my own experiences, and I researched the issues that concerned them in order to lend a hand. I learned a great deal through trial and error as I guided my students in this way. And over time, I noticed that the same issues would arise again and again with each new group of girls who went off to college. Eventually, I got to the point where I had an arsenal of tried-and-true strategies that significantly helped students year after year. I also had an eye-opening realization as to why these strategies were making such a big difference in their lives.

Here's what I learned: I had accumulated more than an "arsenal of strategies." While each strategy I shared was extremely helpful when applied separately, they became much more potent when combined. The girls would apply a strategy, then build upon it with another, and another…until something remarkable would occur. Students would reach a point where they had assimilated a simple – but powerful – system for orchestrating their own success. It's not that these students weren't capable in the first place, but with the help of having this "system" set up, they ramped up their college success to an entirely new level. From that moment on they would have a much more meaningful – and enjoyable – time at college. In fact, they went on to achieve more success than they ever thought possible!

It was so exciting! Proactively building upon the strategies in this way had set students up for a huge payoff: it instilled in them a dramatically effective – almost magical – system they could use to accelerate their own college success. And once students mastered it, they could keep using it for the rest of their lives.

This "magical college-success system" had such a huge impact on the lives of my own students, that I was determined to share it with as many college girls as possible. So I did what any good teacher would do: organized the strategies and broke this incredible process down in a way that would be clear and accessible. I became passionate about giving more students the chance to discover how very simple it is to enjoy a much richer college experience… and life!

And that's what I've been doing ever since: getting this information into the hands of as many students as possible. I'm thrilled that I've had the opportunity to connect with students worldwide, through a variety of vehicles and formats. And now – finally – I'm sharing this life-changing information right here in this book.

I invite you to take a deep breath and get ready to feel more confident, purposeful, and inspired. You're going to undergo an eye-opening transformation as a result of reading this book.

That is my gift to you.

Part I

Discover
The 5 Must-Know
Secrets

Introduction

Five Secrets to make you SHINE in College

First of all, College Girl…Congratulations on being a college student! Whether you've just recently started school, have been there for a while, or are about to begin… you're on an incredible journey! I'm so pleased this book ended up in your hands because it will enhance that journey and help make this exciting time in your life even better!

That you've made it to this point is a huge achievement. After all, considering all the time, effort and preparation it takes just to get into college, you've accomplished quite a feat! And you know what? Successfully navigating your college journey is another feat unto itself.

Naturally, there are many compartments in the life of a college girl, and getting all the pieces to fit is a gradual process. College academics are challenging. The social scene takes figuring out. Sports and many other extra-curriculars add more layers to your busy and demanding life. Factor in the fact that you may be living away from home for the first time. Then multiply it by decisions such as what to choose as a major, whether to go Greek, study abroad, take on internships, what you want to do after graduation. (☺h, and, naturally, you'd like this whole experience to be fun, too!) College epitomizes the proverbial balancing act. It takes practice, finesse, a proactive approach, and a crash course in time management.

It's all very exciting, and – honestly – it can also become overwhelming. It's so worth it, though, to master the college-life balancing act. There's nothing quite like the satisfaction that comes from truly excelling in college, while still having fun making memories that will last a lifetime.

> But how to do it all? How to make it work so that you get the most out of college? How to get to the point where you SHINE – both inside and outside the classroom?

Through trial and error? Well, yes! Of course. That, after all, is a great part of the adventure!

But as you navigate your own journey, allow me to reach out with some crucial information that will make a huge difference to your overall success and happiness at school. A friend once told me you have to learn from mistakes… preferably other people's! Well, as a mentor to college girls for many years, I – along with the students – have learned a great deal through trial and error. And I'm pleased to offer you the opportunity to benefit from this experience.

There are plenty of ups and downs in the life of a college girl (sometimes all in one day!). But what we've discovered is – no matter what issues you encounter at school, you'll handle them far more skillfully once you know five very helpful secrets. Time and time again, these secrets prove to be a complete game-changer for students I mentor. In fact, they make such a difference in students' lives that I wish the secrets were mandatory curriculum for every college girl today: they are without a doubt "Must-Know Secrets"!

Once you add them to your own life at college, you're going to find that everything falls into place much more smoothly for you. In fact, you'll begin to realize that you've discovered a secret weapon that will help you every step of the way through college. What is this secret weapon? Think of it as a "Magic Wand" that you can wave whenever you need it. And when you do, you'll find it much easier to –

- ★ get everything done,
- ★ overcome stress,
- ★ attract great friends,
- ★ excel in your classes,
- ★ avoid the weight-gain,
- ★ truly enjoy yourself,
- ★ achieve all your goals,
- ★ and more.

In short, knowing the 5 Secrets gives you a Magic Wand that enables you to handle college life with much more ease and skill. And not just college. You'll be able to use this Magic Wand to accomplish all that you truly want in your life… for the rest of your life! Not a bad concept, is it? Well, it gets better.

The good news: it's incredibly easy to apply the 5 Secrets and get that Magic Wand working for you. That's because you already have the potential – RIGHT NOW – to access it. (Unfortunately, for some people that's all they ever have: the potential to access it.) But YOU are going to discover how to…

★ First, realize the potential you have to access your own Magic Wand.

★ Next, learn how to access it.

★ Then, practice using it.

And once you do, you'll have found yourself a secret weapon that will be yours for the rest of your life!

I've already helped countless college girls discover their own Magic Wands. And it has changed their lives forever! I use mine all the time, yet it continues to amaze me and to enhance my life every day.

I'd so love YOU to access yours, too — as soon as possible – and start benefiting from the power it will bring to your college experience!

ARE YOU READY?

First, take a moment to create a picture in your mind of your very own Magic Wand, one with a beautiful STAR on the top. (Make it gorgeous!) Okay, great. Now expand that vision to include the location of your Magic Wand. It's conveniently located... right inside of you. Try to picture it there. Really see it within you, lying dormant, just waiting to be utilized, just waiting to bring you... whatever you wish!

That was pretty easy, wasn't it?

NEXT, YOU ACCESS IT.

Now that you've had a glimpse of your Magic Wand, the way to take hold of it and put it to work for you is to fire it up. The brighter it is, the more powerful it becomes. So, you're going to ignite that beautiful STAR on top of your Magic Wand. (Take a moment to picture that as well. Envision your Magic Wand inside of you with the STAR on top completely illuminated with brilliant light.)

Now, here's how you'll make that vision come true: you'll ignite the STAR on top of your Magic Wand one section at a time. The STAR has five sections, right? Well, each time you learn one of the 5 Secrets, you'll be lighting up one section of the STAR. Five sections of the star. Five Secrets. By the time we're through, the entire STAR will be illuminated.

And it gets even better: As you light each section, you'll find you become more and more energized by the experience. You'll reach a point where your Magic Wand starts to fire-up automatically. The igniting process becomes unstoppable. (And so do you!)

Let's have a look at that STAR on top of your Magic Wand:

Each section represents an important component of your life at college: **Strength, Instinct, Mind, Soul,** and **Body**. And as we unlock the Secret for each of those sections, your Magic Wand will ignite.

Every section of your STAR plays a crucial role in this incredible process:

★ **The bottom two sections** – Strength and Body – provide a solid foundation that will support you in college.

★ **The two side sections** – Instinct and Soul – provide you with inspiration and rejuvenation.

★ **The top section** – Mind – keeps you in the proper mindset to shine – in every aspect of your college life.

When all five sections work together – that's when the "magic" happens!

> **The harmony of this alliance ignites your STAR to full BRILLIANCE, And you've got yourself a powerful force: YOUR VERY OWN – useable – MAGIC WAND!**

Each STAR section is in synch, propelling you towards the achievement of your goals and giving you what feels like "magical power" to overcome obstacles you encounter along the way. This process will enrich your college experience. As you unlock each Secret and fire-up each section of your **STAR**, you'll become inspired and your life at college will be more joyful and meaningful. What's more, you'll begin to **radiate brilliance**, attracting people to you before any words are spoken. It will shine right through you, all from the power of your Magic Wand.

Sound too good to be true? Let's move along, so you can see for yourself! And you can start radiating **brilliance** as soon as possible!

It's Time to Discover the 5 Must-Know Secrets!

Part I

I'll reveal and explain the 5 Secrets in Part I of this book. Each Secret will correspond with one section of that STAR you're about to power up on top of your Magic Wand. Although we'll examine each Secret individually, keep in mind that they're fluid. That is, each works in harmony with all the others. So, I would suggest as you read Part I that you simply **take it all in and allow yourself to grasp the big picture.** (You'll have the opportunity to synthesize and apply what you've learned in Part II.)

To help you get this overall feel for the 5 Secrets, I've included stories and tips from recent college grads. (In a few of these anecdotes, I've changed names at the students' requests.) In addition, I've also added some enlightening reflections from not-so-recent grads. These contributors were kind enough to share how the 5 Secrets affected their own personal experiences from college. You'll find these stories at the end of each section.

I invite you to curl up, relax, and enjoy Part I as your overview of the 5 Must-Know Secrets.

Part II

Once you get to Part II, you'll be ready for the **5 Must-Know Secrets Action Guide** where you'll have the opportunity to begin applying the 5 Secrets to your own life at school. Here is where I'll review specific Action Steps and get you started on them. I also provide space for you to write your own reflections, respond to questions, and keep track of your progress. I've laid it out simply and succinctly for you; I know how busy you are. A huge benefit of the Action Guide is that you'll get to see first-hand how you can fold the 5 Secrets right into your college life. They won't get in the way of your active schedule. They'll simply enhance it.

OFF WE GO —

Hold on to your vision of the Magic Wand inside you as we take a closer look at each of the five sections of its STAR. Get ready to feel confident, empowered, and inspired!

Get ready to… SHINE!

First Star-Section: STRENGTH

Secret 1

**Discover and explore your unique core gifts.
Their Strength is the foundation for your success.**

Section One:

**"Being at college is only the opportunity.
You – and you alone – will determine the result."**

Steve — Western Michigan University

In our senior year of high school, my friends and I created our own "clubhouse" of sorts in the basement of one of our homes. We adorned its walls with colorful neon signs, holiday lights, photos and other memorabilia. The room was divided into sections. We had some beat-up sofas and chairs in various sitting areas and a pool table in the "games" section. Way off to one side was an old mahogany trunk. It stood all by itself in a dimly lit area. And as the year progressed, that old trunk began to play a major role in our lives, mine in particular.

Twenty or so of us would gather at our "clubhouse" regularly on weekends, usually inviting guests to come hang out with us. We shared many a laugh that year and generally had a blast in our festive headquarters. Of course, being seniors in high school, each of us also experienced our respective emotional low points from time to time along the way.

It was because of these low points that old trunk came to be known as "the psychiatric trunk." You see, often I would find myself seated on top of it as one of my friends confided in me about this boyfriend/girlfriend challenge or that BFF squabble. I would listen closely to each person's concerns, then offer support and suggestions. Mostly I'd empathize and try to cheer the person up. I didn't mind listening to my friends' woes. In fact, I found it gratifying to know that I was able to lift their spirits when they were down. I actually remember a number of evenings when there was a line of people waiting to sit beside me on "the psychiatric trunk"!

Well, I didn't go on to become a psychiatrist when I grew up. But had I known then what I've since learned, I would have made note of what my experience on "the

21

psychiatric trunk" revealed about me. You see, we all possess something called core gifts. They're our innate talents. Often these core gifts are such a part of who we are that we don't recognize them as gifts at all. They come so naturally to us, we simply don't see them as anything out of the ordinary.

What I didn't realize from my experience at the time is that I'm naturally empathetic and am drawn to opportunities to help others. I didn't see it because that quality is as natural to me as the nose on my face. But it also happens to be an aspect of what makes me uniquely who I am. Now I realize – and I understand why – I'm happiest in a career that calls upon me to use this innate ability.

Your Core Gifts

You, too, have your own core gifts. And the more you get to use them, the more passion you bring to whatever you do. Also the more you use your core gifts, the **happier** you are in what you're doing. That's simply because when you're passionate about something, you tend to enjoy doing it!

So what does all this have to do with college? Excellent question. And it happens to have two answers:

> **1)**   College offers the perfect opportunity for you to discover *your own* core gifts.
> **2)**   The sooner you uncover them, the more you will truly *enjoy college*!

That's where this **First Star-section – STRENGTH – enters the picture**. Now is the time to learn how to identify your own core gifts and to keep track of them. Would you believe that only 20% of the population is passionate about what they do for a living? Discovering your core gifts will help you find your passions, so you can be one who loves what you do. The more you uncover your unique talents, the more proactive you can be when it comes to choosing classes, a major, and possible career. You'll be on your way to loving college (and the rest of your life) when you begin to uncover your own core gifts!

It's actually an exciting process. It doesn't happen over night, but it's fun – and eye-opening – once you get the hang of it. So why not begin right now? You'll be amazed by what you learn about yourself! Here's how to get started.

How to Uncover Your Core Gifts
(Remember, you'll have the opportunity to write and keep track of your Action Steps once you get to the Action Guide in Part II.)

First, Look Within Yourself

Core Gifts
Action Steps

1) Reflect upon what activities you enjoyed as a child. Ask yourself what you particularly liked about them. When you were younger, what did you think you wanted to be when you grew up? What themes emerge for you when you think back on your younger years in this way?

2) Begin to tune into what is joyful work for you, what gives you the greatest pleasure. Usually it will be what causes you to lose all sense of time as you are engaged in it. Notice when you are naturally focused and not easily distracted. Remember what you were doing last time you felt inspired.

3) Regularly ask yourself, "If I could be doing anything in five years, what would it be?" Answer the question honestly and write down your responses. It sounds obvious, but it should be a proactive practice that you do often.

4) Keep a list of your natural abilities as you become aware of them. You won't yet know how it will all fit together in your future. That's okay. Keeping track of what inspires you will help you tremendously as you navigate your college years.

Second, Look To Others

You'll find it enlightening to ask people who know you to weigh in on this topic, as well. It may seem strange to ask others questions about yourself, but it can really inform the process. Your most powerful gifts are often ones you don't even realize you possess! You'll be surprised what people may realize about you that you haven't yet.

Ask Them to Answer These Questions:

1) What do you think I do naturally well?

2) What 5 words come to mind when you think of me?

3) What would you call upon me to help you with?

Look for **common themes** between *your own* personal assessment responses and the ones you receive *from other people*. Remember that your core gifts may seem so natural to you that you've never stopped to consider them gifts at all. *They are*…and uncovering them will help you tremendously as you proceed with your college experience.

Third, Approach College as an Explorer

Continue the process of uncovering your core gifts as you participate in activities and classes at college. Realize that you have natural abilities that you're here to use, and they will be the ones you enjoy doing the most. *So approach college as an explorer.* As you try different experiences, pay attention to what inspires you.

I worked with a student, Krystal, who took an oral interpretation class as part of her college's distribution requirements. When we were evaluating what her core gifts might be, Krystal described the experiences she had preparing her presentations for that class. Apparently she would practice in front of the mirror until she felt each presentation was ready. She said it always *seemed* like she had been rehearsing for about twenty minutes. But time and time again, when she checked the clock afterward, she'd be shocked to find it had been more like two hours! The time flew by for her during those practice sessions. And she always did extremely well on the presentations in class. Krystal learned from this experience that she has a natural talent – and passion – for presenting in front of a group.

While she had no interest in being a performer, she made note of this core gift. When considering careers, she had important information to add to the equation. Krystal realized she would enjoy a job that required speaking in front of groups. This information helped her tremendously in choosing a major and future career.

Krystal ended up going on to business school. After graduation, she worked for an executive training firm. Her specialty became helping executives improve their presentation skills. Eventually, she and one of her colleagues opened up their own – very successful – training company. She loves her career, and it all started by giving herself the chance in college to discover one of her own core gifts!

> I switched majors half way through my academic career. It paid off for me because I chose a major I would love and excel in and I did! I went from a Business/Marketing major to a Journalism/Speech Communications major. After changing my major I excelled on the student newspapers and became the religion editor. I also won an award for my column, Foundations of Faith. If I stuck with Business/Marketing I would still be in school right now and probably not doing too well. (Renee, Houston Baptist University)

You won't discover the ideal job to woo
Until you uncover what's unique about YOU.

The more you allow yourself to be an explorer, the more information you'll have to help you keep track of your own interests. Keep an open mind; you have much to uncover along the way. Dabble. Begin to get a feel for what subjects resonate with you. Look at your college courses as an opportunity to learn about the subject matter and more about yourself. Most schools give students a grace period before they have to commit to the classes they will take each term. Sign up for more classes than you'll actually take and then drop the one or two that aren't piquing your interest.

As you learn more about your core gifts, you can choose classes and activities that allow you to practice using those talents in order to strengthen them. The ones that tie in to your natural abilities will help you improve upon what you already do well.

Hmm...I'm Not Getting an "A" in This!

Naturally, during your exploration, you'll find that you won't excel at everything you try. Simply expect that to happen and don't let it disappoint you when it does. The reality is the challenges will offer valuable lessons in your assessment of your natural strengths. Simply consider each experience a helpful opportunity and move on.

Choose something you want to learn about that interests you. You don't have to be really good at whatever you choose, just be curious. (Taryn, Radford University)

I chose to major in Journalism but I never wanted to be a 'journalist.' I looked at that program objectively and realized it would set me up for a career working for myself better than just a basic BA in Business.

Through journalism, I learned to write, copyedit, draft and distribute press releases, design for print and digital media, write marketing and business plans, sell advertisements (and likewise, buy advertisements) set my own deadlines and project schedules.

I think many college students look at the degree by the name only. They think 'Journalism, oh, that's if you want to be a journalist,' when in reality, it's just the opposite. I now work for myself and own several different businesses and my degree in journalism helps me every day.

If you think about it, a degree in business doesn't teach you to write. Likewise, a degree in English doesn't teach you business. Both of these things are vastly important to practically any career, so I always suggest taking a few journalism classes at the very least. (Cole, Marshall University & University of Cincinnati)

Avoid getting bogged down by your GPA rather than inspired by what you're learning. If you do poorly on an assignment or test, don't obsess about your average. Instead look at it as a positive opportunity to find out what you aren't yet grasping. Go in to see your professor and find out what you did wrong. Ask questions until you learn what you need to know. There are many reasons for getting a low grade, the least of which has to do with intelligence. Sometimes you're inspired and in the flow with an assignment, and you get an "A." Other times you think you're in the flow but have missed the point of the assignment and don't fare as well with the grade. Or you'll be overtired and perhaps more focused on a different course. Resist seeing your grades as a reflection of how successful you can be in your life. Keep the goal of learning as much as you can from each class and don't obsess over your GPA.

As an explorer, you'll find that some of what you're figuring out happens through process of elimination. It's helpful, then, to also pay attention to what you don't enjoy doing, so you can potentially cross it off the list. It's all worth it, though, because one of the greatest experiences at college is to discover you have a passion for a particular subject or field. And often it's not what you originally expected!

So, survey the terrain, make note of what you discover, and then keep moving ahead with your new knowledge to guide you.

Vocational Tests

As you continue viewing the smorgasbord of college through the lens of an explorer, you may find yourself interested in vocational tests. After all, part of what you're figuring out is how you might tie your abilities to a possible major and future career. I know many students take these tests at some point during their college years. No reason not to look into them.

It's worth mentioning, though, that vocational tests are not the "be all and end all" to lead to your "perfect" college major or career. You are unique, so no standardized test is going to give you all the answers that pertain to you and you alone.

It was my experience to never trust what other people said about a professor or a class. There were a few times when my classmates complained that a certain course was far too hard or that a particular professor was a harsh grader.

In several of these instances, I took those courses or professors because I wanted the challenge. What I found was that they weren't really harder than anything else but rather they required you to be more engaged in the class and really participate. You couldn't just sit back and go unnoticed. It was in classes like those with professors who truly cared about personal interaction that I learned the most. (Nancy, Quinnipiac University)

You can certainly give them a try, however, to see what you find out. You'll learn about categories of skills and some careers that utilize those skills. Keep in mind if you take these tests, that answers can be skewed according to any preconceived notion you may have at the time. If you've got a certain career in mind, you may not even realize you're answering the questions with a slant to that present career goal. So you may want to take these tests at different times along the way. And always view the results with a grain of salt (i.e., don't take them too seriously).

If you're interested in checking them out, your school's Career Placement Office will probably offer these tests. You can also search "Vocational Tests" on the internet and find plenty of options from which to choose.

Skills You Acquire Along the Way

Of course, in addition to keeping track of your natural gifts and abilities, you'll also want to *acquire skills* along the way that may not come as naturally to you but will help you in your future career and in your life. A skill is an ability that comes from learning and practicing something. For example, regardless of the major you choose, you will likely benefit from having strong **computer** and **writing skills**. They will help you enjoy more success in any number of careers. You'll also do well to have some basic *business courses* under your belt. Who knows? You just may find yourself taking whatever career experience you've garnered down the road, and going out on your own as an entrepreneur!

Keep a list, then, of your core gifts **as well as other skills you acquire at college**. When you do, bear in mind that the skills you bring to the job market will usually fall into three categories: Physical, Mental, and Interpersonal. All are helpful for doing a job well.

> **1) Physical skills –** motor related talents that you do with your hands or body.
> **2) Mental skills –** cerebral abilities that are more analytical in nature.
> **3) Interpersonal skills –** social talents that cultivate personal relationships.

So, as you're keeping track of your gifts and skills, make a note of which category they fall under. Are you a great writer? If you have beautiful hand-writing, that's a "physical" skill. If you're talented at writing research papers, that's a "mental" skill. Whereas, if you make it a point to regularly write text messages to stay in touch with friends, that's an "interpersonal" skill.

There are two skills in particular that you'll want to master in order to excel in any career: Time Management (Mental Skill) and Getting Along with Others

(Interpersonal Skill). They're also vital for enjoying success in college. If you practice them now, you'll not only get up to speed for your career, but you'll have much more fun at school. We're going to take a closer look at both of those skills right now. (You'll find it helpful to review them and keep track of how you're doing with these important skills in the Action Guide in Part II.)

Skill #1

Time Management

In college you're responsible for planning your own time more than ever before. Now is the perfect opportunity to master the art of time management. Take a look at the following action steps, and you'll be on your way to making this vital skill one of your strengths!

Proactive Time Management Action Steps

1) Schedule your free time. Rather than the other way around, actually decide when you're going to relax, have fun, etc. Then school work is what you will do the rest of the time.

2) Keep up the momentum between classes. Instead of having to stop and start again all day long, keep going, so you're in a proactive groove. When you have a short block of time available, you can review notes, read a short article, run errands, or e-mail a professor. Make your days productive. You'll get much more done, and you'll stay alert and motivated.

3) Learn how to be a smart studier. You'll be inundated at times with reading assignments, and frankly, you won't be able to read every word. Check out chapter and section headings first to get an overview of the topics. Then skim certain parts while reading some sections more thoroughly. You'll get a sense of what works best for each class as you go along.

4) Take advantage of meal time. "Breaking bread" with your friends is fun and a great way to beat stress, but you don't have to eat every meal together. You might want to get used to eating one meal by yourself each day. Have it in the dining hall or bring it outside, to your room or some other quiet place. Bring some reading with you or notes to review and use the time to accomplish something. Then you can really appreciate your social meal times when you have them.

5) Speaking of your room, don't study there. You'll get much more accomplished in the library. That will leave you more time for socializing, relaxation, and other fun activities. It can take students their entire freshman year to figure out that they accomplish much more when they go to the library to study. You can get a head start by getting into this habit right away. Better to save your dorm environment for fun time.

6) Make your own deadlines. You have much more freedom with your schedule in college, which means you have much more responsibility to figure out when you're going to get assignments done. Although a project may be due in two weeks, you'll need to add more deadlines to that time-frame, your own deadlines. Otherwise two weeks becomes this ambiguous, extended, unproductive period and before you know it, you've come to the point where you're one day away from the due date with nothing yet accomplished.

7) Plan backwards. No matter what the assignment, work backwards from the due date and make some headway on it every step of the way. If you have a test in three weeks, create chunks of study time well in advance, so you're working towards the test date in preparation. Don't plan to study for the test for the entire day before it takes place. Try to avoid doing anything in its entirety right before it's due.

When it comes to managing your time, it helps to look at the academic part of college as your "job" at the moment. By proactively planning how you'll spend your time, you'll be amazed at how efficiently you'll "take care of business," and have plenty of hours for FUN!

Part of that "fun" will be making friends, certainly a highlight of the college experience! The second skill worth polishing in college will help you with that undertaking… and much more.

My biggest challenge was fitting everything I wanted to do into my schedule. I enjoy so many things, and I had belonged to so many different organizations in high school, it was hard to choose what I really wanted to do.

For example, I was a hardcore athlete in high school as well as a devoted actor. I knew that I ultimately wanted to act, not play sports. So I majored in theater and communication, but I still played intramural sports. If you have a lot of things you want to do in college, my best advice is to prioritize, map out your classes for the four years you will be there, and get a really good day planner because you will live by it. (Krista, Loyola University Chicago)

Skill #2

Connecting with Others

For most of you reading this book, your friendships from high school were many years in the making. You may have close friends you've known since kindergarten.

Now you're in a different environment. Suddenly you have all these new people around you, and of course, you want to settle in with a group of friends as soon as possible. You're going to find wonderful friends in college. Some you'll meet early on and know for all the years you're there. Others you'll connect with along the way.

Being in the unique position you're in – pretty much starting from scratch with college friendships – offers you a valuable opportunity. That is, it's a chance to sharpen your interpersonal skills, something you'll find hugely beneficial to your career success as well as for building a circle of friends now.

Getting along well with others opens doors...

It helps with College Survival 101 – whether it's getting along with roommates, professors, fellow teammates and club members, or finding yourself a great circle of friends, you will enjoy your college life more if your interactions are positive.

It also helps you thrive in your future ... because regardless of what career you end up pursuing, the better you are at connecting with others, the more effectively you will network in order to secure a job and to excel in it. The number one method for finding a job is – and probably always will be – through networking. So, the better you are at connecting with others, the more success you'll have.

(And let's face it: given the choice, wouldn't you rather have people like you?)

Here's the key — **if you make people feel good about themselves, they will want to be around you.** They'll be drawn to you intuitively, often without even realizing why. By incorporating the following action steps into your regular interactions, you'll begin to find people are naturally drawn to you.

Forging Positive Connections with Others
Action Steps

1) **Face the Person** – Your body positioning is an important factor in making a dialogue exchange positive. Turn towards the other person and lean ever-so-slightly in her direction. Avoid crossing your arms in front of your chest.

2) **Make Eye Contact** – What color are your roommate's eyes? How about the students' across the hall? Your professors'? Make it your goal to find out! Always look into someone's eyes upon meeting him. In fact, try to be the first to establish eye contact.

3) **Enjoy the Interaction** – I don't care if it's "Word!" or "Whazzup?" or "It's nice to meet you" (depending upon your personality and whom you are meeting). Whatever words you use, let the person know you're happy to meet him through the upbeat sound of your voice. Feel happy to meet new people and you will sound welcoming.

4) **Use Names** – Make the effort after you learn a person's name to use it! That way the new name will pass from your short-term to your long-term memory. Whenever possible, envision a person you know or someone famous who has the same name as the person you're meeting. Then think of something they have visually in common. If you allow that visualization to enter your mind, you will have a much easier time remembering the new person's name the next time you meet her.

5) **Remember Your Goal** – Connecting with people you meet doesn't mean you're inviting them to come to your home for summer vacation. You're just getting acquainted. Avoid making judgments, just engage. It's not a competition; it's an interaction. Smile!

6) **Show Interest** – Being interested is actually more important than being interesting. The fact is most people love to talk about themselves. Use this information in your favor. Use it to remind yourself not to go on and on about you! (Yes, really!) And let others talk about their favorite topic: themselves! So, ask open-ended questions. Then respond by showing you're listening and encourage them to tell you more.

7) **Be Upbeat** – See these connections as positive opportunities. Even if you're having a challenging day, make your goal be a positive spin. For example, when someone asks you how you're doing, you might respond, "Actually, I'm having a day of mishaps, so let's focus on something good

31

that happened to YOU today." This strategy results in a win/win: you get a reprieve from thinking about the day's challenges, and the other person gets to talk about herself.

8) **Pick up on Cues –** While you're actively listening, notice the other person's conversational style. The most obvious qualities are volume, speed, and degree of animation or energy. As you pick up on these cues, subtly alter your own patterns to harmonize with the person to whom you are talking. For example, if your new acquaintance speaks rather softly, tone your own volume down as well.

9) **Keep your Cool –** Ask other people questions and be tolerant of differing opinions. You'll rarely persuade others to change their opinions anyway, so enjoy the art of a good discussion while respecting another's point of view. People have different ways of looking at things for all sorts of reasons. That's life. Don't frustrate yourself by feeling you have to get everyone to your "side." They're not enemies; they're just part of the patchwork of the world. You'll feel much more empowered at the end of a conversation if you make it a practice to respect the people with whom you are conversing and keep your sense of humor.

Ideally these nine steps should happen quickly and simultaneously. And you're in the perfect environment to **practice them** with so many new people around you! Obviously, you're not going to end up best friends with everyone you meet (nor would you want to). But once you incorporate these steps into your natural repertoire, you'll be blown away by all the positive connections you make. It's great for the ol' confidence, too.

You have an incredible opportunity at your fingertips to excel in **time-management and connecting with others.** Be patient with yourself because you're simply not going to get it right every time. But, right now, while you're in college, is the ideal time to practice!

When you approach college as an explorer – and practice these vital skills as part of the process – you uncover a great deal of information about yourself. And when you combine your core gifts with the skills you're acquiring along the way, that's when you begin to discover who you truly are and the unique qualities you bring to the world!

In Summary

First Star-Section: STRENGTH

Gifts + Skills = Strength!

To discover what's right for YOU, keep track of —
1) Your own core gifts,
2) Skills you acquire along the way.

The more you allow yourself to be an explorer, the more information you'll have to help you keep track of your unique STRENGTH. So survey the terrain, make note of what you discover, and you'll be that much closer to falling in love...with the rest of your life!

In the next Star-section, we'll focus on what you can do with all of this fascinating information you're learning about yourself!

But first, more insight on **STRENGTH...**

Reflections on Strength

"I Wish I'd Been More of an Explorer of my Inner-Self..."

Upon entering college, my goal was to become a lawyer because of watching shows such as *L.A. Law* and *Perry Mason*. I wanted to be the next Grace Van Owen and become a partner in a major law firm.

I became an English major in order to accomplish this goal. Even though I was doing well in my English courses, I did not feel energized by Shakespeare and Hemingway. During my second semester as a freshman, I took a history course and became passionate about the subject. As a history major, I had the opportunity to research, write, and present my findings. The development of these skills made me feel that I was on the right path to becoming a lawyer. During my senior year, I applied to law school and was accepted into American University's Washington School of Law. *And after all that...* I decided not to attend American University. **I didn't want to go to law school after all!**

That's why I wish I had been more of an explorer of my *inner-self*. I had always liked reading, writing, and researching. However, I lacked the confidence to say that this was truly my passion. Also, I had been told by others that this was not a "realistic" career and that you could not make money doing it. Because of my lack of confidence, I let my career choices define me rather than having the strength to make decisions based upon my inner-self.

I also wish that I had been more of an explorer when it came to keeping track of what my professors were discovering about me. Many of them had identified my natural core gifts. And those professors had recommended that I pursue my Ph.D. in history because of my academic achievements. However, my mind was consumed with becoming a lawyer. Now, when I reflect on my desire to become a lawyer, I realize I was only concerned about impressing others.

I had always been told that poor decisions can bring learning opportunities. By making a poor decision, I did learn about confidence. I also learned to not be overly concerned about what others think. In addition, I learned about the importance of having a contingency plan. In college, I did not participate in any of the career fairs. As a history major, I did not pursue my teaching certification because I "just knew" that I was going to law school. If I had done some of these other options, I could have been better prepared when I decided not to go to law school.

Fortunately, I was able to find a job and attend graduate school. I did eventually follow my passion in life. I have taught courses at the community college and college levels in American History, World History, African American History, and European History. I'm currently creating a nonprofit organization that teaches youth about career development, skill assessment, and self-assessment. I have authored two books. I have been asked by schools, churches, and organizations to speak on the subject of history as well as on my book *I Can Do Anything*.

Even though I was able to ultimately pursue my passion, I don't recommend this type of journey to discovering your core gifts and talents. Instead, I urge you to be an explorer of your inner-self. Don't wait to assess your skills and talents. Take advantage of the opportunity to be an explorer right now! And, finally, consider the following advice:

1. Choose a major that highlights your core gifts. You can only determine your core gifts through self-assessment and skill assessment.

2. Learn to seek advice. Talk with your advisor and mentor about your core gifts.

3. Ignore the negativity of what others think. You have to be the "captain" of your career. Make the best decisions for *you* in order to live your best life.

4. Do not choose a major or career based solely on money. Do what you love and the money will follow.

Carolyn Mattocks
Author, "I Can Do Anything"
Speaker, Colleges & Conferences
B.A. History, North Carolina Central University (Summa Cum Laude)
M.P.A., Public Administration, North Carolina State University

Upon entering college, I knew exactly what I wanted to study, major in, etc. My counselors and mom thought that was an ideal plan as I would be able to graduate in 4 years and have a very linear plan of my academics. One of the risks I took was straying away from this pre-determined academic plan and taking classes that solely interested me. Surely, if you're constrained financially or have other competing factors, you have to balance the two, but it is so highly recommended to take classes out of sheer curiosity. College is about learning, so regardless of what classes you choose, you'll benefit no matter what.

(Jessica, University of Oregon)

"Because I was an explorer, I found the perfect path for me…"

During my freshman year, I was on track to be a double language major, Russian and German. I've always loved studying languages. I studied Russian and German throughout high school and had planned on continuing them. I also added in Arabic and Spanish for more fun! I've never gotten such great grades in my life! I was finally able to study what I wanted to!

At some point in my freshman year, I thought about what I wanted to be when I "finally grew up." It struck me. And it struck me pretty hard. I didn't want a job that involved my beloved languages! I didn't really want to be a translator (I'm not a natural at the speaking part of language – I loved the written parts, but written translation jobs didn't seem numerous enough), and I didn't want to be a teacher (I'd taught swimming lessons throughout high school, and while it was okay short-term, it was not my dream).

So when it came down to thinking about what I could imagine myself doing for the rest of my life, I decided that I could see myself being a veterinarian. And here's my biggest piece of advice: If you think you know what you want to do, continue to be an explorer and get a job in that field. I got a job at the Oregon Humane Society to make sure that working with animals was for me. I ended up loving working with animals! I went on to work at two veterinary clinics later on during my time in college. While I didn't end up going to veterinary school (I was much more interested in using natural medicine to help pets achieve health than drugs and surgeries), it led me to the greatest job in the world for me. I'm now an acupuncturist who gets to work with both people and pets, and it's all because I was an explorer – worked with animals while in college – that I found the perfect path for me!

Becca Seitz, MAcOM, LAc
www.ThriveAcupuncture.org

"If I had done a personal inventory of my core gifts…"

I wish I had read Lauren's book before I went to college. If I had done a personal inventory of my core gifts I would have really understood what I was good at and made better choices in my course selections in university. I thought because I had obtained good grades in high school that I had an aptitude for certain subjects. I got high marks in English in high school so naturally majored in English in university. However, I got a rude awakening in my first-year English course. It was a highly competitive field. The reading list was extremely demanding and the essay assignments were more like research papers on other people's work and less on developing my own style of writing.

Looking back now, I realize I was an excellent creative writer. I enjoyed making up stories, plots, characters and sharing them with others, and I was good at it. University-level English demanded a critical and analytical lens that I did not possess. It focused more on creating a logical argument than crafting a creative and entertaining story. I graduated high school with an A+ in English, having won writing awards along the way. But by Christmas exams of my first year of university, I was barely passing English. I felt like a failure and that I had lost my writer's voice.

Had I understood my true core gifts, I would have been able to understand I was an intuitive and creative storyteller. My instinct told me I was in the wrong class, so I dropped English entirely much to the chagrin of my family. I focused on Political Science courses which I ended up majoring in. I did well and enjoyed the learning process but ended up going back to creative writing post- university!

Today, I have written two children's books and created an inspirational series of stories about overcoming adversity called Passwords: Passing On Words Of Wisdom and Hope. My "password" to you is to take personal inventory of your core gifts and try to find out what you're good at and why. Your grades in high school may not be the best indicator of what makes you happy. College is an investment you're making in yourself. So, do take the steps to assess your own core gifts. That's when you'll let your true brilliance shine out to the world.

Jennifer Clark
Life coach, author, public speaker,
Workshop facilitator, radio show host.
www.jenniferclark.ca

Second Star-Section: Instinct

Secret **2**

Follow your Instinct
to recognize the goals and dreams that are right for you.
There you'll find the confidence so vital to your success.

Section Two:

"There is only one way in the world to be distinguished.

Follow your instinct! Be yourself, and you'll be somebody."

Bliss Carmen

Have you seen those inspirational posters that hang on many classroom walls? You know the ones. They say things like **"Reach for the Stars," "Soar to the Life of Your Dreams,"** and – *my favorite* – **"Dare to Dream."** Very inspiring for sure.

But have you ever found yourself perplexed by those posters? I mean, yes, they sound enticing, but what is the "life of your dreams," anyway? And how do you get it? What are the steps? Where's the instruction manual?

Hey, if you knew the answers to all those questions, you'd *already* be waving that Magic Wand of yours! And you'd be on your way to a pretty sweet life.

Well, as a matter of fact, learning the 5 Must-Know Secrets actually gives you a very clear perspective on how to answer those questions.

"Hold on," you may be saying. "I'm not thinking about planning the 'life of my dreams' yet. I just want to have a great experience in college at this point."

Exactly. But what's so remarkable about the information I share with you here is that it will result in your having a much better time in college! Plus you get the added benefit of putting yourself on the path to the life they refer to on those posters…whenever you're ready for that part. Definitely a win/win!

Graduating college doesn't give you all the answers. Instead it gives you a step to reach that next level in your life! (Amanda, Ohio Wesleyan University)

Ever Think About Your Ideal Life?

First, we need to take a closer look at the term "life of your dreams." Think about your own life for a moment. If you *could* have your ideal life, *what might it look like?* Really let yourself visualize the possibilities. Don't worry about the "how" right now. We'll get to that. Simply savor the images that come to your mind when you allow yourself to imagine your idea of a dream-life.

Go ahead. Luxuriate in some beautiful visions of what you might love your life to look like…in college…in five years…in ten years…even twenty.

Inspiring, isn't it?

Now let me ask you: Whatever you may have envisioned, *why* do you suppose you might want those things for your life? What will they bring you? Think about it. What will those images you were picturing give you?

While most people will not share the same dream, they *will* share the same answer to that last question. Can you guess what that answer might be? It's *happiness.* Ultimately, when you envision a "dream life," you're coming up with ideas of what you think will make you happy. *So, to achieve the "life of your dreams," you're really striving for personal, long-term happiness.*

Your Dream Should Make You Happy

You deserve to be truly happy in your life, but that's not something that simply happens. The sooner you realize that fact, the more you can use it to your advantage. You see, you do have the power to orchestrate your life in a way that will bring you that happiness. And college is the ideal place to learn how to start using that power! Since happiness is a goal that everyone shares, it really helps to have a clear understanding of what that word means.

It's interesting – while so many of us want to be happy, few of us actually take the time to learn about the concept of happiness. It would be great if there were courses on this topic in school. Think about it: if you want to be a real estate attorney, you take many classes on that subject until you are knowledgeable enough to work in that career. We all want to be happy in our lives, yet we don't take courses to make us knowledgeable about happiness.

Life is too short to be doing things that don't make you happy. (Megan, Seattle University)

What is Happiness?

Allow me to share a quick overview of this topic as it pertains to your life at college as well as your life after graduation. First, it's helpful to know that you experience different levels of happiness in your life.

The 3 Levels of Happiness

1) **Surface Happiness** – immediate gratification level of happiness. Certain experiences provide a boost of pleasure that is sustained for a relatively short period of time. You might experience this boost when you eat something yummy, have a blast at a party, buy a new fabulous outfit, or receive a witty text message from a cute guy. It's fun. It makes you smile. It's a feeling that doesn't last forever, but it's wonderful to enjoy. *Surface Happiness motivates us to get more of that feeling.*

2) **Glowin' Happiness** – when you're in the flow of doing something you love. You're on fire as you engage in this activity; often it makes you lose all sense of time. It might be playing music, writing poetry, working on the computer, solving a math puzzle, designing an architectural interior, taking and editing pictures, playing tennis. It's usually something that someone else might find challenging, while you take great joy in the stimulation it gives you. *Glowin' Happiness inspires us to create, produce, achieve.*

3) **Fulfillment Happiness** – comes from being a part of a cause that is bigger than yourself. Usually this level entails being involved with an activity that in some way benefits others, directly or indirectly. You feel a gratifying sense of joy every day as a result of your contribution to a community with a higher purpose. *Fulfillment Happiness transforms us from being reliant upon external forces to provide our happiness...to a place where life is a joyful journey that is powered by our own passion.*

Ideally, you'll experience all three levels of happiness in college and for the rest of your life. The first level, "Surface Happiness," is fun and important! It isn't, however, the sustainable type that comes from inside you. In order for your dreams to result in genuine happiness that will be yours for your lifetime, they should also deliver the Second and Third levels of Happiness, "Glowin' Happiness" and "Fulfillment Happiness." They keep the light of enthusiasm in your eyes despite the challenges life throws your way. They give you a sense of joy and purpose that is quite different from the short-term boost derived from external factors.

Now, I'm not suggesting that you need to win the Nobel Peace Prize in order to have a happy life. I am, however, encouraging you to *strive for all three levels of happiness as* you make choices for yourself in college and beyond. How they appear in your life will be unique to you.

Joe, the doorman in my friend's building in Manhattan is the epitome of a happy fellow. Not only is he always smiling, cheerful and upbeat, but he also emits a remarkable energy. One cannot ignore this man's love of being alive. Nor is it possible not to smile, yourself, after interacting with him. I asked him one day about his contagious enthusiasm. He said, "I love my job. I'm crazy about interacting with people. I pride myself in making sure the residents' needs are taken care of. My days fly by. I feel truly blessed to be here and to have this job." The man is glowin' as he interacts with the residents of the building. And he gets fulfillment from being part of a greater purpose, in his case, impacting the lives of those residents. Everyone's dream is unique to that person; it's *the Levels of Happiness the dream produces* that matters most.

Consider this fact!

Lottery winners report being less happy or at the same happiness level a year later, as they were before their megabucks wins! Surprising? Not so much when you consider the Levels of Happiness. Money alone is not the means to those sustainable Happiness Levels.

Napoleon Hill, author of *Think and Grow Rich* conducted an extensive 20-year research project in which he interviewed hundreds of the most successful people of his time. He found that the one thing every person he interviewed had in common was that they were in love with what they did. In fact, his subjects learned that dreams of *fame, wealth and power* resulted in feelings of *emptiness* and often *less financial wealth*. On the other hand, when the dreams entailed being a part of something greater than themselves, the result was *lasting fulfillment* and often *great financial wealth*. The happiest people are deeply committed to what gives their lives meaning.

One way to attract the deeper levels of happiness – "Glowin'" and "Fulfillment" – is to allow yourself to figure out what you can about your core gifts, as described in the First Star-section: Strength. That way you start to get a feel for what might inspire

For Cole, Instinct came into play even before she left for college!

When making the decision on where to go to college, I had four good schools within three hours of my home and scholarship offers from several of them to pick from. I, instead, chose to go out of state to school. I don't think anyone in my family entirely approved of this choice, but I was 100% following my gut feel.

This paid off tenfold for me because I gained legitimate experience in radio (7 national awards and a morning show), met my future husband and got to experience living somewhere else. I now work for myself and own several different businesses.

(Cole, Marshall University, & University of Cincinnati)

you. Consider my example from high school. I experienced "Surface Happiness" from having fun in our "clubhouse" senior year. I found myself completely engaged as I listened to and supported my friends on the psychiatric trunk – I was "Glowin'"! When my friends began to wait in line to sit with me on the trunk, I got a taste of "Fulfillment Happiness" because I realized that I was truly helping them.

So my core gift of empathy brought me the Second and Third Levels of Happiness when I used it to help others. Just this one piece of information (eventually) proved helpful for me when visualizing what *my* "dream life" might look like. As I discovered my other core gifts, I could continue to shape my vision until it became a dream that *felt right* for me.

That "feeling right" part is important to the equation as well. When something you envision for yourself "feels right," your INSTINCT is helping you realize that the vision makes sense for you. And that's the beauty of learning to look within yourself for answers in addition to searching externally. Just as your core gifts are already a part of you, so is the wisdom of this Star-section: Your INSTINCT!

Intuitively, you know more about your future than you may realize. Getting in touch with your own Instinct – and acknowledging what it tells you – will make your college experience more rewarding. It really helps to learn to listen to it.

Your Instinct Will Help You "Dream"

When you're envisioning a possible dream for your own life, allow yourself to truly consider *why* you want it to come true. This Star-section is not about the "how." For now, simply believe that whatever you decide to dream *will actually happen*. What is your *instinctive* reaction? Does the dream you're envisioning for your life "feel right"? Is it really what you want or is it something else? Perhaps you actually desire something deeper that might be better achieved another way.

For example, if you want a particular degree in order to land a specific job, imagine that you have that job already (because you will get it if it's what you truly want, as you will see when you continue reading this book). Ask yourself: Why do I really want it? If it's just to get a paycheck, do some more searching. What is your Instinct telling you? A paycheck means security, but is that job the only way to achieve that security? And at what expense? Does it mean perhaps giving up a more passionate desire that will pay off in more ways? Ask yourself, Is this what I really want or just what I think I have a fairly good chance of achieving? How will you feel once the "Surface Happiness" wears off? Play devil's advocate with yourself.

College is the place to start responding to your Instinct – to listen to your inner intuitive voice – and to consider what will truly make you happy. Many opportunities, both in and out of the classroom, will help you discover your dreams. And they are yours to embrace. So do allow yourself to "listen to your gut" as you carve out a vision of what you want for your life.

Have fun with this process! Luxuriate in the permission you're giving yourself to consider ideas, dreams, and schemes that make you truly excited! This Star-section is the place to try on possibilities so you can figure out what gets you inspired! It's the place to allow yourself to "Dare to Dream," so your true desires can emerge. Enjoy it! Hit the "search for" button inside of you and begin to recognize the files that surface. They're in there. Getting back in touch with your own Instinct – as you consider your Core Gifts and *the Happiness Levels – will help you figure out what is right for you in college…and beyond!*

Dream Your Own Dream...Not Someone Else's

Focus on *possibilities* right now rather than on perceived obstacles. Start to peel off any layers of other people's expectations for you that you realize are not aligned with your own true desires. If you're trying to live up to *other people's dreams* rather than your own, you won't be happy.

Say, "Goodbye!" to any limiting beliefs about what you can achieve and have. The bigger the dream seems to you, the more sense of accomplishment you will have along the way to achieving it and the more interesting your life will be. The bigger the dream, the more passionate you will likely be about it. That's why it's essential that you give yourself permission to go after what *you* truly desire the most!

Staci Spoke Up...
In Response to What her Instinct Told Her

I began college as a business major hoping to go into marketing.
My brother and dad both graduated from the same school with a
business degree. I am not a math person and struggled my first term
with the pre-requisite math courses I had to take. I ended up failing a
midterm and called my dad crying because I was letting him down.

He explained to me that it didn't matter to him what I majored in
as long as I enjoyed it. I finally realized going to college was about
learning about topics you enjoy and are passionate about. That
afternoon I enrolled in the School of Journalism and Communications,
which is one of the top journalism schools west of the Mississippi. I
now work in the field of Health Care Communications and have a
passion for social media. (Staci, University of Oregon)

Molding your vision for your ideal life will be a process…and an enjoyable one. Along the way, though, it helps to practice first with shorter term goals. **Setting (and achieving) short term goals now will really give you a sense of the power you have to figure out what you want… and to get it!** It will also help you to immediately start accelerating your college success. So we'll start off slowly, and work up to even bigger goals… and eventually to waving that Magic Wand of yours whenever you need it! See what I mean by giving the following Action Steps a try!

Dare to Dream in College Action Steps

Start by choosing a short-term goal that you want to achieve at this point in your college career, something that is meaningful to you. It can be any category.

Here are some suggestions:

1) Academic – No doubt one of your intentions in college is to do well academically. As you focus upon that goal, encourage yourself to ramp it up: *At least once each term, choose one assignment and overachieve on it.* Consider the best time to do this depending upon your schedule and other obligations. Then go way above and beyond and knock your professor's socks off.

2) Extra-Curricular – Choose an activity that you really enjoy and *make the decision to accomplish more within it than you originally intended.* If you join the Environmental Club, for example, set the goal to become an officer while you're at college. If you play a sport, plan to surpass a current achievement in some way or go for team captain. The activity you choose is not the issue; it's ratcheting up your intention.

3) Social – If you originally thought you'd like to have one or two really close friends by the end of this school year, raise that desire. Set the intention to have a fabulous group of friends upon whom you can truly rely.

You choose the goal that feels right to you, but be sure to make it one that you'll feel great about accomplishing. You might simply want to do everything you're doing right now…but do it with more confidence, polish and skill. Remember this is the Star-section where you enjoy the permission you're giving yourself to try on possibilities. Choose something you'd be excited and proud to achieve. Once you've chosen your goal, write it down. (You'll find a place to write your goal in the Instinct-section of the Action Guide.)

As we go through the steps together to make your goal a reality, keep in mind that you'll use these same strategies when you're ready to make your *bigger vision for your life* a reality as well! (Your "Dare to Dream" vision.)

Your Dream = A Seed

Once you've determined your short-term college goal, see it as a seed that you will plant right now and watch grow. To help you look at your goal this way, let me explain the analogy.

Think about your favorite flower for a moment. Is it a rose, hydrangea, daisy? Visualize that flower in full bloom, swaying in the breeze among all the other beauties, happy and vibrant. That flower, of course, started as a seed. And once that seed was planted, it was on its way to becoming the gorgeous specimen you're picturing now. The growth cycle was set in place for complete transformation to occur… from seed to flower. If this transformation were not possible, there would be no seed. What would be the point?

Likewise when you decide upon a goal for something you'd like to achieve in college (like excelling on a particular project academically), you're acknowledging a "seed" of desire that you will plant. It's the same when you carve out a bigger dream for your life; you're uncovering a desire – or "seed"– from *within you.*

Once any seed is planted, you must provide the proper temperature, sunlight, nutrients, and water to allow it to grow. That's what we will do with your goal – the "seed" you've chosen for this Action Step. It's also what you will do with the dream you carve out for your life. You'll nurture it proactively in order to make it happen – to "bloom."

Acknowledge your Dream with Confidence

As you plant the "seed," in this case the college goal you set, tell yourself that it *will* grow. It *will* happen. You won't know at this point *exactly how* you're going to make it happen. That part will come. For this step – the planting of the "seed" – you're acknowledging to yourself that you are setting this goal. Do so with the *confidence* that you can make it happen!

The best advice that I received when I graduated college was "it will work out because it has to." And it has become my personal motto since then. And now that I am finding myself looking for a job and moving across the country, I am constantly reminding myself that it will work out because it has to. (Megan, Seattle University)

When you *confidently* set your goal, you start the process of making it a reality. If you look at your goal as a "seed," then the *confidence* you feel is like *watering that "seed."* What happens next is pretty amazing, as you're going to see with the goal you just set. Just as a "seed" begins to grow after it's watered, the path to achieving your goal will start to emerge and become clear to you, allowing it to grow. The more confidence you can muster when you set your goal, the more easily you'll *see* the path that opens up for you to achieve that goal.

Just as nature aligns with the growth-path of the seed that becomes your favorite flower, it aligns with your own desires, providing the path for you to have what *you truly want*. You need only be *aware* of this fact, and the rest will work in your favor. Don't worry yet about exactly what will appear on your path to achieving your goal. We'll get to that. This Star-section is about allowing yourself to "Dare to Dream," whether it's a short-term college goal or a long-term life dream. It's about carving out a vision of *what you want* and then *believing* that you can make it happen.

Let Your Instinct Be Your Guide

As you carve out your vision of a goal or long-term dream, be sure it's something that truly excites you! Contemplate possibilities, and put them through a Happiness Levels test. Be attuned to your instinctive reaction as you do so.

Happiness Levels Test
Action Steps

Consider the short-term college goal you just set for yourself, and ask yourself the following questions:

> **1) Why is this goal important to me?**
> **2) How will I feel once I achieve it?**

> **Now analyze your responses through the lens of all three levels of happiness. If you haven't indicated that you'll be achieving at least two out of the three happiness-levels, give the questions a little more thought. How will reaching your goal result in your enjoying at least two – preferably all three – levels of happiness: Surface, Glowin' and Fulfillment?**

The more an idea excites you, the more passionately you'll desire it. And the more passionately you desire it, the more clearly you'll see the path to success that emerges for you.

The most passionate dream is one that makes you *so* excited, you're actually willing to *risk failure* rather than not go for it! If you get to that point with a goal or dream, it's like adding Miracle-Gro to that "seed." It usually takes a while to find the dream that excites you to that extent, but when you do, that "seed" begins to grow right before your eyes! You become unstoppable. It's worth noting that people who attain their dream-lives are willing to fail, be ridiculed, and criticized along the way rather than *not* go for it. That's how sure they are that they want their dreams to come true.

> **Achievers take the leap anyway!**
>
> **Once they are on that snowboard jumping over the mogul, achievers focus upon where they want to land, not what's going on when they're in midair.**

If you can develop the mindset that standing before you at college are myriad, exciting possibilities, you'll be on your way to *your* dream-life. Don't measure your successes as much as how often you take advantage of the *opportunities* that come your way. If you get caught up in worrying about failures, you'll thwart your possibilities for attaining your dreams. Instead, simply keep asking, "What's next?" *That* will sustain your momentum.

Aim high so that you start to ignite the passion deep within you. Remember, the more excited your dream or goal gets you, the more clearly you will see the path to make it happen in your life. You've already taken a big step by making the decision to attend college. Don't stop there. Reaching your long-term objectives, whatever they may be or become, involves setting and achieving short-term goals along the way. So start right now — choose a short-term goal to reach for now, even if it feels like a bit of a stretch, but one that really excites you! You're going to love what happens next!

In Summary

Second Star-Section: INSTINCT

Tune into Your Instinct!

Allow yourself to "Dare to Dream" and then pay attention to your intuitive response. This Star-section is not about the *how*; we'll get to that. It's about the **what** – enjoy the experience of asking yourself, "**What** do I *really* want?" Your Instinct will help you awaken to goals and dreams that are uniquely yours. Consider all three levels of happiness – Surface, Glowin' and Fulfillment – as you contemplate your dreams and goals.

Reaching your long-term objective starts with setting and achieving short-term goals along the way – so begin by setting a short-term college goal right now and then write it down with the *confidence* that you will achieve it (even without knowing exactly how). Together we'll go through the process to make it happen.

I can already see the first two Star-sections igniting on your Magic Wand. In the third, we'll uncover the next step to getting you what you want!

Reflections on Instinct

"I set the goal to do everything I possibly could my senior year to send us over the top…"

Like many students entering college their freshman year, I wanted to get "involved." Since there was no Greek life on my campus, I joined cheerleading, a women's service club and a fledgling business organization called Students in Free Enterprise (SIFE). I met new friends and filled up my student social calendar—all great things, but I had no idea that the leadership, teamwork and business skills I would gain from SIFE would truly shape the professional woman I am today. I was just following my Instinct.

The goal of every SIFE team is to teach educational projects about business to their communities and beyond. After each school year, regional champion teams from more than 120 colleges present their projects and compete at the SIFE National Competition. My tiny college team managed to get 2nd place my junior year, narrowly and sadly missing its chance to attend the prestigious SIFE World Cup. That experience appealed to all three Levels of Happiness for me. And from that moment on as new team president, I set the goal to do everything I possibly could my senior year to send us over the top.

I quit cheerleading. I quit the women's service club. I even broke up with my boyfriend! At the time, that seemed like the biggest risk to take! My SIFE team and I spent almost every waking hour together planning projects, preparing for competition and really bonding as a group. After tons of hard work, some fun and a lot of lost sleep, the risks paid off. I'll never forget standing with my jaw on the floor when "little Flagler College" managed to win the SIFE National Championship! My alma mater didn't even have a football team, so imagine our shock when our tiny business organization brought home the college's first national title.

The SIFE win literally started my career (I was offered a marketing job on the spot by one of the judges!), brought national notoriety to a little known school and allowed me to leave college on the highest note possible. I definitely felt that the risks I took were worth the reward; but even if we hadn't won, I think I would have been satisfied, graduating knowing that I did everything I could to try…and that's what really counts!

Michelle E. Olson-Rogers
PR Account Director
The Lane Communications Group
www.thelcgroup.com

"It would have given me the confidence to trust my Instinct…"

Now 34, how I wish I had a book like this half-a-lifetime ago when I was 17 and entering college. It all makes so much sense! I spent four-and-a-half-years in college majoring in Secondary Education. If I had a book like this in college, it would have given me the confidence to trust what my Instinct was telling me I really wanted.

In high school I gravitated towards English/speech classes and took almost twice the units we were required to have for graduation. I was a member of the Forensics team and jumped out of bed enthusiastically early Saturday mornings (and I'm not a morning person!) to go compete at speech meets. I received awards at tournaments and qualified for state.

In college, I joined "Business Professionals of America." When we went to State Leadership Conference, I excitedly signed up for an event called (back then) Verbal Communications/Extemporaneous II, which is a fancy way of saying "impromptu public speaking." I received 1st place in the state of Kansas in this event & represented my tiny community college at the National Leadership Conference in Nashville, Tennessee in May of 1995. I had to wonder if it wasn't some amazing beginner's luck when I received 1st place in the NATION beating out those from the expensive private institutions. I decided to compete in the same event my sophomore year to "defend my National Championship." I received 1st place in the State of Kansas again! Off to Nationals I went, and I was stunned to receive 1st place in the NATION for a second year in a row!

Although by this time I had declared my education major, in the back of my mind I dreamed of "really" being a public speaker, delivering keynotes to corporate America, college students, associations and health care facilities. If I had known about the Instinct Star-section back then, I would have declared to everyone sooner what I really wanted for my dream-life: to be a self-employed (oh, the risk!) public speaker vs. teaching in the public or private schools.

As Lauren says in this Instinct section, your dream should definitely make you happy. I'll add to that – you never know what twists and turns life has in store, so do what makes you happy now. Prioritizing your happiness does not make you selfish! I've certainly learned that: On Wednesday, March 24th, 2010 I was diagnosed with Stage Four Non-Hodgkin's Lymphoma Cancer at the young age of 33! My diagnosis helped me find my life's purpose of blending my gift + skill of speaking with this very personal experience. I have now achieved happiness of the deepest-fulfillment-level through launching my brand "Cancer with Joy" to help others from diagnosis through treatment!

If I had known this would happen to me at such a young age, I would have prioritized my happiness more, trusted my Instinct, and given myself permission to say "THIS is my real dream for my ideal life." The fact is (and I love this quote): "If you're interested in something, you'll do it when it's convenient. If you're committed to something, you'll do it (period)!"

Joy Huber / Cancer Survivor, Award-Winning Professional Speaker, Author of "Cancer with Joy" & Professional Coach
www.CancerwithJoy.com
www.JoyHuber.com/contact

"I wished I could just win the lottery and start my own business…"

When I began thinking about choosing a major during my freshman year, my motivating factors were money and prestige. At the time, the career that I thought would make the most money was a doctor so it seemed a "no-brainer" to pursue a biology/pre-med degree. During my first two years, I was very successful in my classes but I had no real interest in or passion for medicine. I continually gravitated towards jobs and volunteering experiences that involved working with children.

The course of my life changed during an organic chemistry lab. Incredibly frustrated from breaking my third Erlenmeyer flask of the semester, I told my lab partner that I wished I could just win the lottery and start my own business working with children. He asked me why I didn't just start my own business without winning the lottery. The idea of taking a risk to start a business without having financial security was an idea that I never entertained but, at that moment, I realized that it wasn't an impossibility. The next day, I changed my major to my true passion, education. I find that the best decisions that I have made in my life have also been the scariest—this decision proved to be both.

I now own a successful private tutoring business. My sister, who I also consider to be my best friend, is my partner. It is the ideal work situation. It required a lot of work, motivation, and belief in ourselves, but it was so worth it. If I could pass along one piece of advice, it would be to pursue what you are truly passionate about even if it is risky or a little outside the box. You never know what will happen until you try and there really is no price tag that you can put on loving what you do!

Amanda Medders
Founder, Tri-Ed Tutoring
www.tri-edtutoring.com

"Everyone else seemed to be having a blast, but I wasn't ..."

When I graduated from high school, my parents couldn't afford to send me to the small, private colleges I wanted to attend. At least, not for all four years. So they made me an offer: stay in-state for two years at a public university with school and state scholarships; then transfer to a different school for the final two undergrad years. I agreed, and chose Florida State University in my hometown of Tallahassee. I based my decision on the practical benefits of a good scholarship, a good education, and a good friend to room with. At the time, it seemed like a reasonable compromise. My parents suggested I look at other state schools because they knew I'd been looking forward to leaving my hometown. But since other people I knew loved FSU, I figured it would grow on me. I should have listened to my parents and followed my Instinct to leave my hometown.

It didn't take long to realize that FSU wasn't the right school for me. From student life to academics, nothing excited me. I often felt frustrated, and sometimes even depressed. I didn't feel like I fit in at the school. Everyone else seemed to be having a blast, but I wasn't. My surroundings were too familiar – from the scenery to the climate – and I often felt like I'd never left high school. I had high expectations for college, and this wasn't the fun and exciting experience I'd hoped for.

Luckily, I did make some close friends. And these friendships are what I attribute to getting me through one of the most difficult phases of my life. Despite my overall disappointment, I kept my chin up and put my energy into doing things that would keep me somewhat uplifted: I hung out with my friends, took day trips to the beach, went on camping trips, worked out at the gym, walked, and even took a pottery class (which I discovered I loved!). I focused on my studies and made the effort to enjoy any good times I had.

It was when I took a leap of faith and signed up for a study abroad program in France, however, that everything began to change for me. Fnally, I was responding to what my Instinct had first told me – to go somewhere new. In fact, that decision marked the beginning of my new and improved college career. A semester in Paris and a summer of backpacking adventures through Europe truly inspired me and brought me back to life. Upon my return from Europe, I was ready for the next pivotal moment of my college career: my transfer to a new school!

Fall of my junior year, I transferred to The Colorado College and my college transformation was complete. I fell in love with the school and everything it offered. I found myself surrounded by things that inspired me: mountains, nature, an open-minded student body, a non-traditional class structure, block breaks, dinner parties and people who shared my values, and who, like me, were enthusiastic about everything the school had to offer. I no longer had to make such a conscious effort to stay engaged and energized; it simply happened naturally. At CC I felt more alive than I ever had, and I thrived. Just walking to class could replenish me if I was tired or stressed-out because the mountains in the distance reminded me of how happy I was to be there.

In the last semester of my senior year I took a Tai Chi class. The class introduced me to meditation, a practice that would not only get me through the writing of my thesis, but through many difficult phases of my life. It was a fitting end to an incredible college experience.

I'm now a life coach and meditation instructor. Knowing what I know now, I'm sure I could have found a school somewhere in Florida that was both affordable and interesting to me. Chances are I wouldn't have transferred to another college if I'd made a different choice at the onset. But at the time I didn't know how to evaluate my choices. I didn't understand the importance of following my intuitive desire to leave Tallahassee. My Instinct was spot on – I needed to go places and do things that made me feel truly alive. If I were to give one small but essential piece of advice, it would be this: in college and in life, do things that inspire you!

Paige Continentino
Life Coach and Meditation Instructor
www.paigecontinentino.com
www.meditationfortheimagination.com

"It came only through following my Instinct and sticking to it..."

When I entered college as a freshman, I had no idea what I wanted to do with my life. I knew I loved to write but, I did not know what type of career I could have with it, except be a journalist. It took me three years to finally find a major. However, through the process I learned very quickly that sometimes as you're following your Instinct, it's just as important to recognize and embrace the things that you don't want for your life.

I started out as a Journalism major, then realized that I don't like writing for print. I switched to an English major and realized that I had had my fill of Shakespeare. I switched to graphic design and realized that I had no drawing skills. It wasn't until an advisor suggested that I take a film class that I discovered my true calling. It was a perfect place for me to put my creative writing skills into play. After that one class I was hooked, but it came only through following my Instinct and sticking to it, even when I wasn't sure which direction it would take me.

Deciding on a film career was only half the battle. I had to settle within myself that my path in life was not going to look like others. A filmmaker, or any artist for that matter, typically cannot look in a local newspaper and find a job. I got into the habit of making a goals-list every year. I would only list about five goals that were manageable within a year's time. This helped me to visualize what I wanted my life and career to look like.

Every day I would make a confession that I had accomplished the goals on my list. Then, mid-year I would take myself on a retreat – which usually consisted of locking myself in a room for a day or checking into a hotel for a night. I would reflect on how I was progressing with my goals. If I was lacking in any area I would create an action plan to get back on track. By the time I graduated from film school, I had finished shooting two feature films and several short films and commercials.

Before I knew it, I was experiencing a happiness that I only dreamed about. And that happiness continued after grad school when I transitioned into becoming a film professor. It's very fulfilling to work with young people who are looking to find their place in life. I definitely concur: you must follow your Instinct, even when you're not sure where it will take you!

Avril Z. Speaks
Film Director & Associate Professor, Howard University
www.azuspeak.com

Third Star-Section: Mind

Secret 3

**As you envision yourself achieving your goals,
use the power of your Mind to keep negative energy
from sabotaging your success.**

Section Three:

"The only place where your dream becomes impossible
is in your own thinking."

Dr. Robert H. Schuller

> **Did you know...**
> ...most people use only about 10% of their true potential?
> That's right! And what's so ironic about this fact is that it goes against
> our basic human Instinct to strive to be all we possibly can!
> Do you know the major reason people don't use their full potential?
> They think themselves out of it!

It's true. Most people begin with excellent intentions. Then along the way they begin lowering their expectations for their lives. Their Instinct could inform them that they're settling for less than what they really want, but they're not paying attention to their Instinct. So they settle. And, unfortunately, they end up with this nagging feeling of disappointment that keeps them from ever being truly and completely happy. At that point, they're often not sure why they're in this predicament, but they don't know what to do about it.

Don't worry. You can keep yourself from falling into that trap once you understand this Star-section. Not only will you be willing to confidently admit to yourself what you truly want, but you'll know how to make it happen! That includes keeping it from NOT happening, which is a step unto itself, as you will see (and the key to Secret #3):

Third Star-Section: MIND

Discover its Power!

Think about the short-term college goal you set for yourself in the last section. When you envision yourself achieving that goal, does it excite you? The more excited you are to achieve it, the more passionate you'll be about going through the steps to make it happen. That's important because – on the other hand – the more of a stretch the goal is, the harder your Mind will try to "think" you out of it! We're going to keep your Mind from stopping you in your tracks on your path to getting what you want! Instead, we'll capitalize on its power to help you achieve your goal.

Your Mind has tremendous power. You can succumb to its power to keep you from achieving. Or you can utilize its power and achieve what you want. The decision is up to you. But first you have to know how your Mind works or there's no decision to be made!

Just as a star is powered by intense natural light, you possess your own internal energy that radiates from every part of you. Everyone carries energy around inside of them. You undoubtedly pick up other people's energy quite often. For example, if one of your friends is down in the dumps, you can often sense her mood even before she tells you about it. That's no coincidence; you're sensing her internal energy. It radiates from inside of her, just as yours does from inside of you.

Even the thoughts in your Mind have their own energy. And that energy is at your disposal! You have the ability to use its power to orchestrate what you want for your life. And to do so isn't so much a matter of trying harder, either. To utilize the power of your Mind to help you rather than to get in your way, you simply need to change how you think.

 ~ The "Seed" Analogy ~

When you utilize the power of Your Mind, you're providing that seed (goal) you planted with the proper temperature it needs to grow all the way to maturity and to bloom.

Temperature is not a constant; you have to continuously gauge it. The same is true with your Mind. Once you understand its power, you'll need to regularly gauge it – to be sure YOU are controlling and utilizing that power rather than allowing IT to control you.

Here's an example that may clarify what I mean by changing how you think:

> ### Consider this –
>
> One day while out walking my dog Piper, I stopped to chat with a friend. After a few moments, Piper began to bark. I looked down and saw that she had walked around a fire hydrant, looping her leash around it in the process. Now she wanted to get back to my side but couldn't because there wasn't enough length left on the leash for her to reach me.
>
> All she had to do was walk back around the hydrant the way she had come, and she could have made it to my side easily. Instead, she began trying to stretch the little bit of leash she had left in order to get to me. Going back the other way would have been so easy. Whereas trying to get to me by tugging at the leash was never going to work, no matter how hard she tried.

Okay, I realize Piper isn't a person. But, still, the example holds true: all she had to do was change how she was thinking rather than to work harder. Tugging against that leash was a futile waste of energy. When you change how you think, you utilize the power of your Mind to help you achieve your desire. (In Piper's case, that's pretty much to be by my side every second of her life.) When you change how you think, you set yourself up to avoid the trap of settling for less than what will make you truly and completely happy.

The sooner you realize how to utilize the power of your Mind, the more satisfaction you'll get from your college experience. No matter what comes your way at school – day-to-day, month-to-month, year-to-year – your knowledge of how to utilize the power of your Mind is going to help you. Period.

Let's take a look at three specific examples of how to harness the power of your Mind in order to bring you more success…and get you what you want! To get a sense of the difference these strategies will make to your life at college, you're going to practice them with the short-term goal you set when reading about the Instinct Star-section. As you do so, you'll see that slightly altering how you think will pave your way to achieving that goal. Then you can continue to use the same strategies to achieve more and more goals. Until, eventually, you'll see first-hand that you can absolutely "Dare to Dream" because you know how to accomplish what you set out to achieve.

Okay… on to those strategies.

3 Strategies for Utilizing the Power of Your Mind

1) Negative Energy Control

2) Mental Imaging

3) Momentous Living

Stay focused on your short-term college goal as we take a look at each of these powerful strategies!

Utilize the Power of Your Mind

Strategy #1 – Negative Energy Control

Are you more of a glass-half-full or glass-half-empty kind of girl? I had a friend in high school who actually campaigned to win the yearbook classification "Class Pessimist" senior year! He knew he fit the category, and figured it was his best shot at getting his picture in the superlatives section of the yearbook. He won, but – in all honesty – I can't imagine that this particular trait has served him very well in his life.

Generally speaking, we all move back and forth between optimistic and pessimistic perspectives, depending upon the situation. Those people who are fortunate enough to be natural optimists live their lives with a distinct advantage. People who are more positive tend to be happier and more successful. On the other hand, those who put a negative spin on the events of their lives are more apt to get stuck and find themselves frustrated and unhappy.

There are a few reasons for these differing outcomes:

1) As long as we are more pessimistic in our focus, the energy we radiate will be predominately negative.

2) When we send negative energy out to the world, that is exactly what we get back in return: negative results.

3) On the other hand, when we make our focus more positive, we invite success and happiness as a natural way of life. We bring the positive results to us!

Now, you may be thinking, "sure that makes sense, but how much control does a person have over whether she is optimistic or pessimistic?" Well, here's

It may sound cliché, but you have to put yourself out there and try new things.

When you challenge yourself in college, you'll be amazed at the results! (Meghan, Eureka College)

the exciting part – you absolutely DO have control over which type of energy you allow into your life. You have the power at your disposal to shift your own energy to a more glass-half-full mindset, which will help you tremendously to achieve success! Doing so simply involves gaining a clear understanding of the energy at play inside your mind. Then you can practice how to use its power!

A Look at the Two Sides of Your Brain

First, it helps to consider how your brain enters into this energy discussion.

RIGHT BRAIN – is the side that welcomes experimentation and creativity. It springs into action when you tap into your Instinct and allow yourself to Dare to Dream. It's inspired by that short-term college goal you've just set for yourself.

LEFT BRAIN – loves safety. It tends to freak out when you take a step toward implementing an exciting idea for your life and will try to shut down the experimental side as a way to protect you.

KEEP BOTH SIDES HAPPY – When you recognize this opposing dynamic, you can calm your left brain down by acknowledging it's trying to protect you. You can inform it about a change, so it's less stressed by it.

I have a friend who takes huge leaps of faith in his life (right brain) and enjoys great success as a result. I love the expression he uses as he embarks on a new, exciting journey: he calls it "scary fun." My husband and I now use that phrase to acknowledge both sides of our brains as we move forward on a new endeavor.

Another friend of mine listens much more to the safety messages from her left brain. She had a very tough time when she decided to retire after a 30-year career in the same job. It took her months of counseling to convince her safety-loving left side that all would, in fact, be well in this new chapter of her life.

The Energy Dance

Just as you have two sides of your brain – left and right – you also have two opposing "voices" regularly dancing around each other inside that active Mind of yours. One is predominantly negative while the other is more positive. These two voices reflect the differences between the two sides of your brain. The negative voice stems from fear (more left brain) while the positive voice is more encouraging (right brain).

Here's the eye-opening part: Without any input from you, the negative voice will usually dominate the positive one! It pushes itself into the spotlight of your attention whenever it chooses. And it often "chooses" to do exactly that, especially when you step out of your comfort zone to do something big, great, new, and/or different. Your positive voice, on the other hand, needs to be encouraged to play an active role in your thought-process. (Yup, you guessed it, especially when you step out of your comfort zone to do something big, great, new, and/or different.) So, to use the power of your Mind to help you get what you want, it's crucial to learn how to make your positive voice more dominant.

Much has been written about the dynamics between these opposing voices inside your mind, and they've been referred to by different names. I call them your negative energy versus your positive energy since these voices are part of your thoughts – and since thoughts have energy. But the bottom line, regardless of the terminology, is this: you'll be happier and more successful when you're aware that these opposing "voices" exist and that you can control the balance between them.

Positive Energy = The Real You

The positive energy – the less assertive of the two forces – is the energy that nourishes the goal that you want to achieve! When your positive energy is dominant, you forge ahead confidently on your way to success. Even when you encounter obstacles, positive energy helps to sustain you, to keep you on track as you move forward toward the achievement of your goal. Want to have a smooth transition to college… ace a project… land that internship… find fab friends… beat stress… ? You need your positive energy to dominate, so it can lead you right where you want to go. Positive energy is a "must have" for orchestrating your college-success.

Negative Energy = A Manifestation of Fear

To a certain extent, negative energy (or N.E.) is natural because, as you know, that left brain wants to keep you free from danger. But it becomes negative energy when those safety messages snowball and turn into poisonous thoughts. It's negative energy that dishes out such messages as, "I can't…, I'm not capable of…, I'm not good enough to…, I'll never succeed at…, I don't deserve…," wreaking havoc on your confidence and self-esteem. These are the exact thoughts that can keep you from getting what you want in college. But you can control these thoughts by changing how you think. And changing how you think entails recognizing those messages for what they are: negative energy trying to cloud your perspective.

Often first-year students fall victim to their own negative energy when they first arrive on campus. The newness of the experience can be daunting, and of course, that's when negative energy loves to enter the picture. One student I know sought my help half-way through her freshman year because she had become completely overwhelmed by her snowballing negative energy. Julia had been top-dog in high school: president of her class, National Honor Society, talented athlete. When she got to college, she was stopped in her tracks by all the other extremely high-achievers in her new surroundings. She was no longer in an environment where she was known and respected – even put on a pedestal – for her accomplishments. At college, she had to start over again, and she began to worry that she wasn't good enough. A sabotaging idea started to creep into her thoughts – that her high school success had actually been a sham all along. Rather than remaining positively focused upon her own journey, Julia's reaction was to be intimidated. Her confidence nose-dived, and she began binge-drinking to numb her damaged self-esteem. After a few months at school, Julia called me, and opened-up about her predicament. She ended her story by lamenting (and pardon this exact quote), "I'm tired of waking up in my own vomit." She had allowed her positive energy to be usurped and had lost her way as a result.

So how do you keep this negative energy from controlling your thoughts? How do you encourage your positive energy to dominate? You change how you think!

To start, it's as simple as learning to recognize your own negative energy as left-brain security warnings gone awry – not truth. All it takes is the recognition that these thoughts are negative energy to move towards allowing your positive energy to lead you to success. When you "hear" messages in your head that you're not smart enough, talented enough, strong enough, pretty enough, rich enough, or in any way deserving enough – you need to recognize those messages as your negative energy rearing up, trying to undermine your confidence.

We all have negative energy that wants us to believe those types of messages. AND WE ALSO ALL HAVE THE POWER TO OVERRULE THAT NEGATIVE ENERGY. But first, we must recognize it for what it is.

Then once you've recognized it, you're ready for the next step to combating negative energy. You're ready to confront it: ASSERT! Even though you won't feel confident at that exact moment, state out loud – "That's N.E. (negative energy) not ME!" Really come out and declare it firmly! This simple – but forceful – act of confrontation will cause the N.E. to weaken slightly, but enough to make room for positive energy to fill in the void.

At that point, think of yourself as driving a car, and shift that car into REVERSE. Back away from those sabotaging doubts, so you can see them for what they are: left-brain security warnings gone haywire. Pulling back from your negative energy (N.E.) makes it easier to identify it as an entity that is NOT WHO YOU ARE but an object to be confronted. And the good news is that seeing it as an object that doesn't define you or even speak truthfully requires an awareness that you do already possess. So the more you confront your N.E. in this way, the more natural the process will become to you. That doesn't mean your N.E. will ever exit the picture forever. But it will diminish and lose its power over you the more you practice dealing with it proactively.

As you begin to confront your N.E. in this way, it helps tremendously if you're aware of an eye-opening truth, especially as it pertains to achieving a goal – Negative energy is often a sign of something good to come! Of course, you'd be more apt to think the opposite would be the case. But here's the amazing reality: the closer you get to achieving something you really want, the more your negative energy will try to dominate your thoughts!

Allow Me to Repeat That!

The closer you get to achieving a goal or dream, the harder your negative energy will try to trip you up!

This information is crucial; it's also life-changing! Once you realize this truth, you will actually recognize your doubts and fears as positive signs that you are, in fact, going to achieve a goal! (And, believe me, it's something you will need to keep reminding yourself of time and time again.)

Consider Julia, who was ambushed by her negative energy when she got to college. She had been looking forward to going to college all through her four years of high school. She had worked hard to get there, too, and had been accepted to a top university. What she wanted, of course, was to do well once she got there. But going to college also meant stepping out of her comfort zone (as do most big, worthwhile, exciting goals). So, when she was the closest she'd ever been to achieving that goal; that is, arriving on campus and finally able to start her college career, what happened? Bam! Negative energy kicked in and tried to throw her off-course.

She and I worked together until she was able to recognize and confront her N.E. That was a huge step forward. At that point she backed away from it and saw it as an object separate from her true self. We changed how she was thinking. Instead of believing those "I'm not good enough…" thoughts, she started to celebrate them. That's right: celebrate. Because she learned negative energy is a sign that she's getting closer to achieving something big in her life. In Julia's case: succeeding at a top college.

This same strategy will work for you, as well. So, the way to change your thinking is to resist the temptation to buy into the false messages. Instead, celebrate the negative energy. "Lots of negative energy? Oh, good, I'm that much closer to getting what I really want!" It's definitely not what your immediate reaction would have been before learning about negative energy. And it's tough at times because – and this is really important to remember – when you're in the grips of N.E., you can really believe its lies.

From Negative to Positive

The first school I attended was small. Towards the end of my first semester it became clear to me that this was entirely too small a school for me. Everyone knew me, and I knew everyone else, which at first was nice but it also opened a lot of opportunities for gossip.

One day I decided that I had really grown out of the university. I decided from that day forward I would try and get into a bigger, more distinguished college.

Getting my acceptance letter to the University of Maryland was an amazing feeling and the beginning of the rest of my life. Making the transition from a student body of 2,400 to 24,000 was tough at first but one I am happy for. I remember one day walking 20 minutes from one end of campus to the other looking around and just smiling the whole way. I was so proud of myself and where I was. It was an amazing feeling.

(Caitlin, University of Maryland, College Park)

Don't give up, though. Keep recognizing it, confronting it, and – yes – celebrating it. It will get easier with practice because you'll see first-hand the amazing results that come from overruling your N.E. in this way. You'll shift from being frustrated, disappointed, and discouraged to confident, hopeful, and inspired. Which would you prefer? Julia chose confident, hopeful, and inspired by proactively confronting her N.E.

Remember, "That's N.E. not ME!" Say it out loud. Be aware of the existence – and significance – of the negative/positive energy dance in your Mind. Also embrace the fact that you absolutely DO have the power to make your positive energy your dominant force.

Other People's Negative Energy

Now that you have a clearer understanding of the role negative energy tries to play in your own life (and the fact that you have the power to overrule it), it's really helpful to keep in mind that it exists in the people around you as well. Even people who seem completely confident on the outside deal with the insecurity that stems from their own negative energy. As a matter of fact, arrogant people – you know those people who intimidate others and make them feel inferior? – are often the most insecure; they're just trying to mask it. Imagine that! Once you realize this fact, it makes perfect sense to make it your personal goal to be **self-assured but humble, rather than arrogant and insecure.** There's simply no reason to allow your negative energy to run your life.

But, since most people aren't aware of this fact, it will help you tremendously to be cognizant of what makes others do the things they do. Have you ever heard this quote by Charles Swindoll? – "Be kinder than necessary because everyone you meet is fighting some kind of battle." Well, apply that concept to your understanding of negative energy. If people treat you badly, put you down, or are just plain rude, your own negative energy may latch on to that behavior causing you to lash out, feel hurt, or worse. (Think of it as your negative energy dancing with their negative energy.) If you recognize negative behavior in others as their **unconscious deferment to their own negative energy,** you begin to look at other people differently, more compassionately.

Making ourselves "right" and others "wrong" is one of the most common behaviors that results from allowing our negative energy to control us. I worked with a group of students one day who began to laugh about a peer, calling her weird. They said, "She stands in the girls' room for the longest time and just stares at herself in the mirror." I suggested that perhaps she was attempting to focus upon her own positive energy, to push through her cloud of negative energy. I asked them what part of themselves they were feeding by putting this girl down and laughing at her. When they recognized that their own negative energy was getting in the way of feeling compassion for this girl's struggle, they changed how they think.

It was a fascinating exchange because it's not the type of thing people usually discuss. But when it was open to discussion, this group of girls became empowered by their realization. They began to grasp the peaceful feeling that accompanies genuine self-confidence. That's when you get to the remarkable place where there truly is no need to put others down in a futile attempt to make ourselves feel artificially – and momentarily – superior.

There are many benefits to consciously overruling your negative energy. At the most basic level, it really builds this genuine self-confidence I describe. It allows you to be completely comfortable in your own skin without having to "prove" anything to others. And that's a great place to be when you're navigating the college social scene.

> In spite of all the stress that comes with maintaining a work/life balance in college - laugh. If you don't feel confident, at least you'll look it - and that's half the battle. A sense of humor is key in any situation.
> (Carly , Binghamton University)

It's also crucial for accomplishing what you want in your life, including that short-term goal you set in the last section. Whenever you start to doubt your ability to accomplish that goal, apply the following Action Steps:

Negative Energy Control Action Steps

1) Recognize It –When you find yourself thinking, "I'm not capable of achieving my goal," for whatever reason that pops into your mind, realize that your negative energy is trying to take control. See it for what it is: left-brain security warnings gone awry (NOT the real YOU)!

2) Combat It – ASSERT! Declare firmly – "That's N.E. not ME!" Say it out loud. State it with confidence! You'll cause the N.E. to weaken.

3) Back Away from It – Create some distance between you and those sabotaging doubts, so you can view them as an object to be confronted, not a reflection of the REAL YOU.

4) Celebrate It – Realize that negative energy is often a sign of something good to come! So, when those discouraging thoughts enter your mind, celebrate the fact that you're getting closer to reaching your goal...and that you WILL achieve it!

5) Laugh at It – Free yourself from the daunting vibe of negative energy by refusing to take it too seriously. Laughter really works; it stops negative energy in its tracks. (Remember, that's N.E. not ME!)

6) Overrule It – The best way to get through a challenge is to keep going! Your positive energy has already begun to take over at this point. Use it to push through whatever challenges you face in achieving your goal.

These Action Steps will prove crucial to keeping you on track to achieve your first short-term college goal as well as anything else you're determined to accomplish in your life. These steps will help you tremendously on your college journey, but so will being kind to yourself. You're going to make mistakes in college; they are part of the experience. Forgive yourself for mistakes you make along the way. Simply view them as learning experiences that take you closer to your reaching your goals! You'll really overrule your negative energy when you take the word "failure" right out of your vocabulary! Keep this in mind: when it comes to reaching your goals, you'll have "successes" and "learning experiences." Those are the only two options.

You begin to take control over the destructive tendency of your negative energy the second you become aware that it exists. It can't control you when you are "on" to it. So now that you know how to overrule your negative energy, let's focus on ways to encourage your positive energy to run the show. That's how you'll get what you want – and have a far better time – in college.

Here are two remarkable strategies that utilize the power of your Mind to stay grounded in positive energy. The more you use them, the more everything else will fall into place for you!

Utilize the Power of Your Mind

Strategy #2 – Mental Imaging

Now that you know your thoughts actually have their own energy, you can probably see the logic in the idea that whatever you choose to focus your attention on actually becomes your reality. Your mind has this power! And it's something that you already experience every day, whether you know it or not. So you may as well use it to your advantage!

Failure? NO!
"Learning Opportunity"

My lack of interest in my classes resulted in tons of "free time" spent drinking. Rather than attend classes and complete homework like everyone else, I constantly missed classes and assignments. My six months of fun caught up with me when I returned from Spring Break to find that I was at risk of being kicked out of school.

I was worried that college wasn't right for me - but that wasn't the case. Like many other students, I had chosen a major that wasn't ideal for me. Once I had changed my major to something more suitable, I immediately saw my grades rise and even enjoyed being in class.
(Chrissy, Drexel University)

Think about it: If you've ever told yourself that you cannot pass a test, won't pass the test, have no hope of passing the test, chances are – you guessed it – you didn't pass it! On the other hand – let's say you need to find a dress for a dance, and you get really excited to go out shopping, knowing that the perfect dress is out there. You simply can't wait to find it. What happens? Most likely, you're going to find that dress!

So why not take advantage of this phenomenon to help you achieve the goal you've set? You can utilize this power by concentrating on a mental picture of what you want. Picture yourself already having accomplished your goal. Really focus upon it, making the image as clear and as desirable as you can. That way you can truly envision it to the point where it ignites passion in you to achieve what you're picturing. This process – called Mental Imaging – propels you from what you want to achieve to what you plan to achieve. The difference between "want" and "plan" is extremely powerful when it comes to utilizing your Mind.

Try it now with your short-term college goal. Take a few minutes to create a mental picture of yourself having already achieved that goal. Let's say you've set the goal to become more involved in the drama program than you originally intended. Picture yourself at the auditions for a play…with yourself as the director! Spend some time with the image until it becomes extremely vivid and desirable. See yourself calling different actors up to the stage. Visualize yourself making decisions as to which ones will best fit the roles of the show you're directing. Spend some time savoring those images.

When you engage in Mental Imaging, you utilize the power of your mind to help you get what you want. (You also keep your focus positive, so you're less apt to allow negative energy to interfere with accomplishing your goal.) As you practice this strategy, you'll find that you have the ability to accomplish more than you ever realized! Try it now with the college goal you've just set. As you do, it's important to return to that picture in your mind as often as possible in order to get the most mileage out of this powerful strategy you have at your disposal! You can do so by taking a few moments to return to that mental picture at some point each day. As an added bonus, try creating a tangible visual to refer to regularly. Try these tangible aids for Mental Imaging:

Mental Imaging Aid: Vision Journals –

Whatever mental image you focus on, you're using the power of your Mind to set it into motion to occur. In college I created a Vision Journal, which is simply a notebook in which you paste photos that symbolize to you any aspect of what you want for your life. My vision journal represented what I wanted for myself after graduation. I pasted photos of female executives on its pages. I knew I wanted to enter the corporate world before pursuing my goal of becoming a teacher. However, I wasn't sure at that point what corporate career I desired. I did know that I wanted to have my own office and an assistant. Not very specific, I know, but that was all I had to go on at the time. So, I began my visualization with this information, and I used the pictures to help me.

My college friends have since told me that we experienced a lean job market when we graduated, a fact of which I was not aware at the time (but undoubtedly one you've been hearing today, yourself). And you know what? Before long I was working among female executives, just as I had pictured in my vision journal. It took a while until I had my own office and an assistant, but I had set the goal and visualized it, and I did achieve that dream.

Mental Imaging Aid: Vision Boards –

Vision Boards are another hugely valuable aid to orchestrating your own success. They are posters on which you paste pictures that symbolize to you the realization of a goal or dream. You then hang your vision board in a place where you will see it each day. I've had students create them to visualize their goals about careers, lifestyle, academics, weight-loss, and of course, romance. From an intellectual perspective, they're wonderful because they appeal to both sides of the brain. Since the boards are covered with images, the right experimental side of the brain is in its glory, excited to move forward toward achieving the goals pictured. The practical left side of the brain doesn't get all stressed out by the movement toward positive change because it doesn't recognize images the way it does words. You get to import vital positive signals to your mind this way without unsettling the left brain.

> **The Course Syllabus**
> **A Friend to Both Sides of Your Brain**
>
> **A smart strategy in college is to regularly refer to the syllabus for each course you take.**
>
> **Your left brain will love the safety of knowing what to expect each semester and when to expect it. At the same time, you can allow your right brain to devise plans for how you can take a unique approach to scheduling your time and how you might overachieve on one or more of your assignments for that term.**

Whatever your goal, create images of yourself achieving it. Really "see" yourself living with that goal having come to fruition already. Make that your regular practice whenever you set a goal – or Dare to Dream – whenever you "plant a seed." You will change your thinking through this process because every time you focus on the mental image of your success – or the actual pictures in your vision journal or on your vision board – you'll ramp up your own positive energy. And that positive energy is what will take you where you want to go and get you what you want!

Utilize the Power of Your Mind

Strategy #3 – Momentous Living

This final strategy for using the power of your Mind is as simple as it is effective. You have at your disposal a switch that you can use to instantly change how you're thinking. That switch provides a natural – almost magical – antidote to negative energy! When you make it a habit to turn on this switch, you'll become an expert at utilizing the power of positive energy to make good things happen for you at college. I call this "switch" Momentous Living; I also call it a life-changer!

Here's how it works: Whenever you become aware that negative energy has overtaken your thoughts, stop and ask yourself this question: "What is good about this moment in time…right now?" Sometimes the answer will be more obvious than others, but there is always something positive about the present moment. It can be as simple as appreciating the warm bed you're sleeping in or the meal you're eating. It can be the "big picture" reminder that you're appreciative to be getting a college education. There is always something to appreciate about the present moment, and the more you practice looking for it, the better you'll get at finding it!

Let's say one of your friends just blew you off to go to the movies with a guy she likes. You may be bummed because you were really looking forward to going out to a party with her that night. You're definitely feeling negative energy dancing around in your mind. Stop! Before you allow that negativity to take over, ask yourself, "What is good about this moment right now?"

Well, at least she texted me to tell me she was canceling. I'm happy for her because she's really into him. I got a lot of work done today in anticipation of going to the party tonight, so I'm glad that work is out of the way. I'm sitting here in my dorm room at college. I'm fortunate to be here. Life is good. I now have the evening free and simply have to decide how to spend it. Found time! That's a rarity in college. I'm going to enjoy this moment right now and then figure out what I will do tonight. I can enjoy a bit of down time by myself, make other plans, go to the party with someone else, etc. (You get the picture.)

Sometimes you may have to push yourself to see what's "momentous" in a particular moment. But really, even in the midst of an exam, you can find something positive in the experience. You absolutely stop negative energy in its tracks when you focus on what is good about this moment in time…right now!

Momentous means important, meaningful, outstanding. And those are words that should describe your life…and every moment in it! The path to achieving your short-term

"Momentous Living"

Once I stopped too late for a red light and ended up right in the middle of an intersection. It was embarrassing. I was stuck there on display as the other cars had to navigate around me.

I decided to try to take a step back from freaking out in embarrassment, so I asked myself, "What is good about this moment?" I thought, no one is getting hurt here; everyone is getting where they want to go, and I'm listening to a great song on the radio. And it worked. I actually began to feel joy in the moment, which really relaxed me. (Maria, Northwestern University)

college goal – and eventually your bigger vision for your life – should be an enjoyable one. Look for what is good about each moment in time, and you will find it. As you do, you'll begin to feel more happiness within yourself and with your life in general.

A "Mind-blowing" Moment

My senior year of college I ended up falling for a guy. It wasn't love, but it was the most I have ever opened up to a guy, and I ended up getting my heart broken. It hurt and it was not always a fun experience, but looking back I am glad I went through it.

Not only did I learn a lot about myself and what I value, I also got one of the most mind-blowing kisses. And every girl needs to have at least one of those in her life. (Megan, Seattle University)

Practice Momentous Living
Action Step

Ask yourself right now, "What is good about this moment I'm experiencing?" STOP. Really think about that question. Now allow yourself to tease out a response.

Start to observe yourself when you begin to buy into your negative energy. You'll notice the types of tricks you get tempted to allow the N.E. to play. Then if you STOP and focus on what's good about this moment in time, you'll keep your negative energy from playing those tricks. You'll be able to avoid its false, misleading thought patterns.

As you practice putting on the brakes within your own mind, you allow yourself to shift your energy from negative to positive. It's so quick; it's so very simple. But the difference that "shift" makes to your overall success and well-being is staggering. It really is like waving a Magic Wand.

In Summary

Third Star-Section: MIND

Discover its Power!

To achieve a goal requires more than hard work. A positive state of mind as you strive to achieve that goal is what delivers success to you. Implementing the strategies in this Star-section will change how you think, keeping that positive energy dominant on your path to getting what you want. The process gets easier with practice. That's why you should absolutely use these strategies to help you achieve the short-term college goal you set in the last section. Now is the perfect time to experience the power of your Mind for yourself.

Keep practicing the strategies in this Star-section. Continually gauge your positive/negative energy balance. Keeping your positive energy dominant uses the power of your mind to help you to attain your goal, not work against you. The more you practice, the more you harness your Mind's power to work for you. You'll become adept at successfully overcoming challenges. And – in short – living your life will become a more enjoyable experience!

Now it's time to prepare to achieve that college goal you've set. In the next Star-section, you'll get set-up for the success that's coming your way!

Reflections on Mind

"This was nothing but negative energy..."

I took my place standing in the long line of graduates. Following in single file I made it to my seat and confidently sat waiting for my name to be called. As I reached for the rolled paper that had previously been tied in a ribbon I was overwhelmed with emotion. Excitement, happiness, relief, pride, and satisfaction, but what I was missing was direction.

Attending college for me was a long battle of ups and downs including pressures, responsibilities, time lines, homework, projects, and high expectations. I spent so much energy fighting to reach my goal of graduation that I neglected to place focus on how I was going to get my message out to the world. I never imagined where I wanted the roads of education to lead me, I wasn't specific – I didn't have a vision.

I felt I was constantly fighting an uphill battle. With every challenge I overcame I was exhausted and I immediately started looking for the next obstacle I would have to tackle. What I didn't realize was that this was nothing but negative energy that was cycling over and over again. I was so busy stomping out fires and moving to the next, I didn't have the time or the peace of mind to contemplate my direction.

I absorbed much later in life the knowledge that every effect, every end result, every emotion, every action – everything starts with a thought. My hindrance was that three quarters of my thoughts were negative, and I hadn't even realized this. Because of this, my struggles were magnified.

Now I understand... how numerous negative thoughts and emotions really are. What gives a thought power is the energy surrounding it. How much energy you give it depends on many different variables such as your past experiences, your beliefs, and even your overall emotional state at any given moment in time. Most people aren't blinded by lack of vision as much as they are by fear and negativity. But not me I was blinded, period.

After I implemented positive thinking in my life and followed the road of my visions, it was a smooth, enjoyable, and exciting journey. I would have graduated and had that much needed direction in my life ten years earlier if only I had discovered these powers sooner.

A good sign to indicate if you are stewing in negative energy is if you notice a feeling of stress, frustration, anger, annoyance, fear, hurt, tension, or helplessness. Negative emotions are caused by negative thoughts.

What I teach now is how to use SOAP to banish these negative stressors from your life. First, you specifically identify your stressor (what is causing the negative thought to occur?). Then, you use problem-solving techniques to determine your options to resolve the issue. Once all of your options are listed, you decide what the most advantageous way to proceed is. And – most importantly - you move forward and take action to resolve it (don't procrastinate).

Specify your stressor

Open your options

Agree on your action

Proceed to perform

You carry a special uniqueness that only you can provide to the world. Nobody can touch lives in quite the same way as you. Positive thinking will help you to grow stronger with every challenge. You will progressively continue to believe in you and your abilities as you develop your skills and master your hidden talents.

Susan Del Gatto
Stress Strategist
www.abc-stress.com

"It wasn't until I learned to quit playing those lies over and over in my head…"

In college, I suffered more at my own hands than I did at the hands of others because I didn't know how to process my emotions and make healthy choices. I really wish I had not believed the lies I told myself.

I believed that no one loved me…false. I believed that no one would notice if I dropped off the face of the earth…false. I believed I messed up everything I touched …false. I believed that I would never be good enough and make the right decisions in life…false. I held onto those false lies until they tore away at me and I began to self-mutilate. It wasn't until I learned to quit playing those lies over and over in my head that I was able to overcome the insecurities and self loathing that I suffered from.

Now I know – and I offer this advice: Be strong in what you know for a fact to be true. Everyone is created with a divine and wonderful gift. Find yours. Find yourself. Find your strengths and emphasize those. Replace those bad thoughts with positive ones so that your wise choices match your positive outlook. Don't let everyone else tell you who you are. Learn to be happy with the person that you look at in the mirror. Make the choices that you need to so that when you do see that person staring back at you in the mirror, you will recognize her and be content with her. Don't sell yourself short. You are worth everything. Let no one tell you any different!

Tracy Lewis
Author, God is Always There

"That's when the negative energy started to kick in…"

When I went to college, I was only 17 years old. High school had always come pretty easy for me so I think I just assumed college would be the same. Plus, in high school, I'd actually had extracurricular activities and a part-time job that helped me lay out my schedule. Once in college, I had three classes in the mornings and then this giant block of time that I didn't know how to plan out.

So, I pledged a sorority without really knowing what that meant and found myself living in a large house with over 100 girls. I had always been pretty independent and pretty confident, but being with such a large group of mostly older girls tested that. That's when the negative energy started to kick in. I found myself worrying that I wouldn't fit in unless I was just like everybody else, that I had to do just what they did, that I needed to be more grown-up (or what I thought was grown-up). I started trying to make sure that I was wearing something similar to what the older girls were wearing. I adopted the study habits (or lack thereof) of some of the girls I considered "cool." And, I went to parties several nights a week.

It wasn't until I got my first quarter grades that I realized what I had been doing was not going to work for me long term. The grades weren't terrible, but they were hovering close to what I would consider average which was not something I was used to. I knew I could do better and, luckily, just seeing those grades snapped me out of my freshman funk and got me back in touch with the person I really was.

I could have used a working-knowledge of the power of the Mind back then. It would have helped me to combat my negative energy, and I'd have been happy with my sorority life AND my grades that much sooner.

Erin Baebler
www.magnoliaworkshop.com

"I was allowing negative energy to overrun my rational thoughts…"

I wish I had known how to not let my negative energy get to me and obsess over my body image. I was so worried about gaining the Freshman 15 and Sophomore 20 that I missed out on fun and experiences with friends. I finally got exhausted from turning down friends, and so my junior year I decided to live life fully. Some of my favorite memories are the late night ice-cream runs and pizza study groups.

I always thought the girls around me were judging and the boys we hung out with would think I was fat. The truth is: my girlfriends were not judgmental; they were just as insecure as I was. And the boys didn't think we were fat...they were happy if girls were paying attention to them! Here's the real key...I did indulge in pizza nights and girl-talk with a bucket of cookie dough, and I didn't gain the weight! I was too busy and active having a great time; it all balanced out. And now I look back and would kill for that college figure.

The bottom line is – when I look back at those pictures from college, I see the smiles and friends, not the weight I was trying to keep off. I was allowing the negative energy to overrun my rational thoughts. I only wish I could have realized sooner to be free of my inhibitions and need to control my weight. Enjoy college life now because it will never be exactly as it is in this moment.

Kristen Lucas
thechroniclesofinfertility.blogspot.com

"The truth is, I think I was too insecure..."

When I was in high school, I was a joiner. I was involved in a lot of organizations: Kickline, Key Club and Masquers (my school's theater club), and more. I was a busy student in school and out - I was very involved in my community's dance school. When I thought about college, I thought about all of the organizations and clubs I was interested in joining. I wanted to get involved!

Once I got to school however, I hesitated. Sure, I joined the theater program there and did some community work - but mostly - I kept to my friends and classes. I look back now and I wonder why. Why didn't I spread my wings more? What happened between my active high school career and my decidedly less active college one? Don't get me wrong, I was certainly busy, but now I think about all the different things I was interested in back then (and frankly, am still interested in now), and wonder why I was so afraid to dip my toe into the water.

The truth is, I think I was too insecure.

I somehow thought that joining an organization where I didn't know anybody, or didn't know enough about the work they were going to do would make me stand out in some terrible way. My negative thoughts were persistent and would cycle through my head. What if nobody liked me? What if I wasn't good at the activities? What if I joined and then it became too much work? What if I wasn't smart enough? I played an endless 'what if' cycle in my head and now looking back, I think that cycle defeated my "joiner" intentions.

Had I been kinder to myself and acknowledged that so much of my college life had gone well - finding friends, doing okay in my classes, joining the clubs I felt most confident in - I might have been more willing to embrace the unknown and expand my horizons and friendships. College can be stressful enough without adding on the stress of beating yourself up. Confront that negative energy and move past it. Be yourself while spreading your wings – that's what I would tell anyone about to enter their first year of college.

In fact, here's an example of how being true to yourself while spreading your wings can help. I was a double major in college: dance and political science. In my dance department, my style of movement was decidedly different than what was the "norm" there. Each semester, there was a dance concert comprised of student created works. Rather than choreographing something that I thought the professors in my department would find acceptable, I used the technique they taught and created a dance that was very much my style. It was definitely a risk. I thought they'd hate it, but instead, it was chosen as the closing number to the concert!

Back then, I was too "in it" to understand the weight of that lesson, but now I get it. I dared to take a risk and it paid off. If my experience can give someone else the strength to spread her wings more and be kinder to herself, then that's good enough for me.

Julie Tortorici
Writer, Producer — On the Leesh Productions
www.bestlaidplansfilm.blogspot.com/
www.whatyoucando365.com
www.julietortorici.wordpress.com/

Fourth Star-Section: Soul

Secret 4

Get ready to "catch" the success that's coming your way through Gratitude and Soul-rejuvenation.

Section Four:

Mind
Instinct **Soul**
Brilliance
Strength **Body**

"Gratitude is the fairest blossom which springs from the soul."

Henry Ward Beecher

You're going to LOVE this Star-section. It's crucial, and it's extremely rewarding! Whatever college goal you set for yourself – whether it's to overcome homesickness, excel academically, start a business on campus – you will reach it if you apply each of the 5 Secrets. So, it's vital that you prepare yourself to receive what you desire. Yes, that's actually a key-ingredient for getting what you want! And it's precisely where the Fourth Star-section – SOUL – enters the picture.

Why do you need to "get ready" to receive? Why doesn't your goal just happen without your "preparing to receive" it? Well, look at it this way: If someone throws a softball at you, you'll be much more apt to catch it if you have your glove on and are in the right position to receive the ball. Same principle applies here. You want to be ready to "catch" and "hold onto" the achievement of your goal when it comes your way!

To get a bit more technical, it's based upon a metaphysical principle that simply can't be ignored when it comes to getting what you want, Sir Isaac Newton's Third Law of Motion. "For every action there is an equal and opposite reaction." Your "action" was to confidently set your goal. Now you need to have your own "reaction" ready and in place. When you follow the steps in this Star-section, you set yourself up to receive the success that's coming your way.

Soul = "Sunshine"
Remember how I suggested that setting your goal is like planting a seed? Well, consider this Section of your Star the sunshine that seed needs in order to grow and bloom.

Think of the feeling you get when you're out in the beautiful sunshine. You're rejuvenated. You're relaxed, exhilarated. The Soul Section of your Star should be all those things...and more!

I really can't say definitively that one Star-section is more important than another. All five work in harmony. I do, however, find that this one is often neglected. An unfortunate fact, indeed, because not only is the Soul Star-section crucial for achieving success, but also it helps you have a much better time overall in college! This Star-section will help you manage the college-life balancing act and beat stress. It will keep you uplifted and energized! In my work as a college-student mentor, I notice that students find the strategies in this Soul Star-section particularly beneficial.

Let's get back to your college-goal now and move you farther along the path to making it a reality! Want to get an "A" in Calculus this term? Find a fun date for the holiday formal? Land a job on campus? You're going to put on that softball glove and get ready to "catch" the success that's coming your way.

How do you prepare to receive what you want?

Two ways –

■ First – Apply the principle of Gratitude.

■ Second – Energize and replenish your Soul.

Read on to take a look at what they are and how they'll make all the difference!

#1 Gratitude
The #1 strategy to prepare yourself to reach your goal is to feel grateful for having achieved it, as if it's already signed, sealed and delivered! Be thankful for having earned that "A" in calculus before you even begin the course! Get yourself to the point where you can feel the pleasure of having already achieved it. Spend some time luxuriating in the joy it brings you. Say, "thank you for this grade!" and congratulate yourself for your success.

Once you set your goal, you must feel grateful that you will achieve it as if it has already happened. Gratitude is a secret weapon. Gratitude waves your Magic Wand.

Attitude of Gratitude
Action Steps

Each morning, start out by being grateful that you WILL absolutely achieve the college goal you've set for yourself. Look in the mirror, smile, and say "thank you" for the achievement of that goal, as if it's already happened!

Then come up with at least one aspect of your life for which you feel grateful. What do you appreciate today? Is it your friends, a professor, your computer, interesting classes, enjoyable extra-curricular activities, health, a "good" hair day? Come up with something.

(Remember you should do this every day!)

Gratitude keeps you energized, and positive energy brings you positive results. Whatever it is you desire, it's due to the happiness you think it will bring you – preferably all three levels of happiness! – so dwell on those happy feelings. Then you'll stay grounded in positive energy...and get those positive results.

Important: Avoid the "Opposite" of Gratitude

(Dwelling Upon What You Don't Have)

Beware the trap of "doing the opposite" of feeling gratitude: To focus on what you don't have or don't want gets in the way of achieving your goal; it only reinforces lack of having. Instead, feel grateful for having achieved what you want as you move forward, and it will come.

I worked with a student who had gained twelve unwanted pounds her first year of college. Kathryn told me that she had been trying to lose this weight for more than a year, but she couldn't achieve her desire. I suggested she create a Weight-Loss Vision Journal. In it she put photos of outfits she would wear once she lost the weight, quotes that inspired her, and statements of gratitude for having already achieved her goal. Once she got started, she had a ball creating her journal. The pictures and quotes she gathered really inspired her. Focusing on these positive reminders of her assured success – rather than dwelling on her frustration over her recent weight-gain – motivated her and propelled her along the path toward her desired outcome. This time Kathryn lost the weight!

When you focus on being unhappy with the present, you waste powerful energy on what is wrong rather than expressing gratitude for the positive outcome that you're going to achieve. In Kathryn's case she was dwelling too much on her dissatisfaction over having gained the excess weight. Her journal inspired her to feel grateful for having lost the weight, even before she actually lost it. And that made all the difference!

To feel grateful for something even before you've achieved it is an act of faith. But you'll find that act of faith easier to muster once you've applied the principle of gratitude and seen it work a few times! As you do, you'll also experience how obstacles along the way can actually be blessings in disguise. So – yes – that means feeling grateful even for those obstacles. Trust that it will all contribute to your success in some way, even if you're not sure how at this moment.

As you get used to viewing your experiences in college through the lens of gratitude, you set yourself up to get what you want. Gratitude opens you up to attract positive energy to come your way. And that, ultimately, is how you'll achieve your goal! You can encourage that process.

Gratitude Action Steps (Continued)

(After you say "thank you" for having achieved your goal and for one thing in your life for which you are grateful, do the following:)

As you look in the mirror, see if you can catch a glimpse of that Magic Wand inside of you. Focus on the STAR at the top, and see it filled with brilliant light. Now see and feel that brilliant light shine right through you out into the world. Take a deep breath. Know that you're on your way to having a productive and enlightening day. Tell yourself, "I will be receptive to recognizing opportunities that come my way today, even ones that may masquerade as challenges."

As you walk to class, make it your intention to feel that brilliant light shine out from within you… and to feel gratitude. Tell yourself that by the time you reach your destination you're going to feel the positive energy that comes to you as a result. You're sending it out; therefore, you're going to get it back.

The more you stay focused on gratitude, the more positive your energy will be. Remember positive energy attracts positive outcomes.

Be prepared for those positive outcomes because they ARE coming! So whatever goal you've set, be receptive to notice signs and opportunities that arise to help you make it happen. They will come. But the point is you have to be open to noticing them, and, of course, ready to say "yes" to them. You simply have to know to expect them, so you're ready to see and respond to them.

Let's say your goal is to make some really great friends this year. After class one day, you and another student start chatting as you're walking out the door. You really enjoy talking with her, but it's pretty quick because you go separate ways once you leave the building. Sign! Feel grateful for the conversation and take it as a sign that friendships are coming to you! Regardless of whether or not you end up friends with this particular person, your gratitude for that conversation sets you up to bring friends into your life. I'm describing a very important energy exchange here. You send it out; you get it back. But you've got a far better chance of succeeding with this exchange if you're open and receptive, if you're on the lookout for what's coming back to you.

My friend Christine Kloser, in her book *The Freedom Formula*, suggests that people pick up pennies when they see them on the ground rather than ignore them as most of us do. She encourages this strategy for people who want to attract financial success into their lives. She explains that by picking up the pennies and feeling grateful for them, you shift the energy and set yourself up to receive. My husband and I gave this idea a try and made a game of it. And – guess what? – it worked! Try it; you'll see what I mean about the principle of gratitude and what it brings to you!

You'll notice your energy shifts as you make gratitude a regular part of your life. And as you do, you'll attract the positive energy you need to achieve your goal. Remember that your lens of gratitude should include being grateful for having achieved your goal, even before it happens! It should also include being grateful for each step of the way every day. That leads us to the second aspect of this Star-section:

#2 Keep Your Soul Replenished and Energized

Balance. Ultimately, that word epitomizes the art of navigating college-life successfully. At times you may find your social life is full to the brim, and it's tough to fit academics in there at all. Other times you'll be so inundated with responsibilities, you'll realize you haven't had time to socialize in a while. Well, friend-time definitely falls under the category of "things that rejuvenate you," so navigating that balancing act is important. Also on the list of things that rejuvenate you is time for you – and you alone – to recharge the ol' battery. Alone-time is a rare occurrence in college, but it does give you a chance to catch your breath!

The fact is we all benefit from having ways to stay positively energized. That positive energy helps us to be productive as well as to stay healthy. In fact, a growing number of medical schools now include courses on spirituality as a way of pointing out the connection between physical health and soul nourishment.

Females especially need to get used to this idea of replenishing. We are naturally drawn to giving of ourselves in order to help and nurture others. It's vital that we allow it to be just as natural for us to receive. Otherwise we tend to pay the price for our generous spirits by running out of energy and even getting physical symptoms.

Another place females tend to shortchange ourselves is when it comes to believing we deserve to take the time to be kind to ourselves. If anything we're more likely to be tough on ourselves than to love ourselves. As you know, our "negative voices" thrive on spinning negative energy around in our heads. One result is that we become disappointed in ourselves, damaging our own self confidence. Stress is a huge trigger for negative energy; it's also many college students' constant companion. Lack of sleep is another attractor to negative energy. In fact, there are myriad aspects of college life that beckon to negative energy like sharks to blood.

That's why it's so vital to clear it away by allowing yourself to replenish your Soul. You'll keep your energy positive and stay confidently on the path to achieving the success you seek!

Here's how to do it —

Top 10 Ways to Keep Your Soul Energized in College!

~ #10 ~
Establish a Positive Environment for Yourself

Your dorm room or apartment should provide you with a comfortable space that will have a positive effect on your mood. You want to feel recharged when you're in it.

Warm the atmosphere by having incandescent lamps rather than the cold, fluorescent overhead lighting found in most rooms. Choose (soft, comfy) blankets, pillows, and other room accessories in colors you love to help set an inspirational tone. Hang posters and pictures that you find uplifting. One or two plants that are easy to maintain can add very positive energy to a room.

And don't overlook the benefits of hanging some inspirational quotes on your wall, mirror and bulletin board. They can literally make the difference between a frustrating day and a purposeful, energetically-charged day. (If you want some quotes that will really inspire you at school, I suggest you subscribe to my "Monday Motivators" at CollegeGuidanceGuru.com. Each week you'll receive an uplifting quote that will help keep your energy positive.)

During four years of college there are definitely times a girl just feels bad. There are so many things that can go wrong – and believe me I went through them all! I learned some great ways to get out of a slump.

Here are my top picks. Take a walk, go out to a field and pick flowers, bake something delicious, call a friend from high school and talk for hours, buy watercolor paints at the store and just be a kid, write in a diary, listen to music, get coffee with a friend, buy a new set of pens, get a mani and a pedi, grab a dorm buddy and do each other's make-up, get dressed up for no reason at all, play a board game, eat sushi, curl up with a shameless romance novel and a mug of hot chocolate – and if NONE of those ideas work – every girl knows nothing cures a slump like some good, old-fashioned retail therapy!
(Jessica, Wichita State University)

~ #9 ~
Create a "Dear You" File

You will have plenty of ups and downs in college, sometimes in just one day. Often all it takes is one encouraging word to get you back on track. But – oh – to get it when you need it!

An excellent solution is to keep a computer file of compliments people give you and achievements you feel particularly good about. You can add to it whenever you feel inspired, upbeat, motivated, and especially happy or excited about…well, about YOU.

When some aspect of your life is really going well, take a few moments to write down your positive thoughts. You will love the way this file rejuvenates you as time goes on. Call it "Dear (Your First Name)" and set it up as a letter to yourself. You'll find it tremendously inspiring to read these letters when you're in need of a boost.

It doesn't take long to quickly add a new entry, and you'll be building a composite of yourself that will help you in many ways over the years, including helping you discover your core gifts, decide upon a major and choose a possible career. Most important, though, referring to this file from time to time will help to keep your Soul energized, sustaining you on your path to success.

~ #8 ~
Find a Spot

Have your own special place you go to get away from campus life and replenish your Soul on a regular basis. Find your own spot where you can take a break from the hectic pace of your life at college. It should be a place that makes you feel good — away from your dorm room and from the rigors of studying in the library — a place that doesn't remind you of school.

Your purpose in going there is to take a break from the minute details of your daily life and to contemplate the bigger picture once again. Sometimes all you'll need to do is spend time there in order to nourish your Soul. Simply shut your eyes and allow yourself to feel the positive energy inside you, feel its warmth. You'll benefit if you can allow yourself to "escape" to your special spot at least once a week.

If you're in the dorms, you're often sharing a room and constantly surrounded by people. On my campus I found a bench that was a bit tucked away. I would go there for serious conversations, if I needed to cry, or to go read. Someplace to really call your own will always help you. (Jessica, University of Oregon)

~ #7 ~
Breathe Mindfully, Listen to Guided Inspirations

People are fond of giving this advice: "Don't forget to breathe." And it happens to be good advice. But have you ever wondered about these words? I mean, after all, breathing is an involuntary action. It's not like you're going to forget to do it, right?

Here's the thing about breathing: Yes, your natural breaths keeps you alive, but they don't replenish your Soul. In order to get that added benefit, you need to breathe more deeply, allowing the oxygen to fill your lungs and clear the pathways. You take nearly 30,000 breaths each day, so you may as well make some of them do more than just keep you alive. Deep breathing – also called Mindful Breathing – helps boost your body's immune system and combats stress. It also energizes your Soul.

Students with whom I work find Mindful Breathing clears away sadness, frustration, fear, and irritability, feelings that can lurk just under the surface in the daily life of a college student. They report a new sense of well-being and happiness as a result of this deep breathing technique. (For instructions on how to do Mindful Breathing, see Appendix A in the back of this book.) Some colleges offer yoga and meditation classes, and if yours does, I encourage you to try them, as well.

Another hugely beneficial soul rejuvenator is the Guided Inspiration. It's a relaxing, spoken-word recording that you can listen to at your convenience to give you motivation and encouragement. I suggest students have Guided Inspirations readily available on their computers and MP3s, so they can benefit from the positive energy those recordings provide. (For details on how to access a Guided Inspiration, see Appendix B in the back of this book.)

~ #6 ~
Write in a Journal

When you're upset or trying to figure something out in your life at college, try writing in a journal. Do a freewrite; that is, write down whatever is on your mind for a few minutes without stopping. Don't worry about grammar, punctuation, or spelling; they only slow you down. By writing non-stop in this way, you allow yourself to get to the heart of what's on your mind.

Follow up that entry with a question. Ask a question about whatever you might be grappling with at the moment. Then answer it! Simply start writing an answer, and you'll be amazed at how accurately you'll tease out a response. Let yourself write the answer without stopping, even if it seems like you're getting off topic. Write your response for at least five minutes. The longer you write, the more your answer will reveal itself to you. You'll find this type of journaling incredibly empowering.

~ #5 ~
Find Mentors, Coaches, and Master Minds

I became very close with my Public Relations Professor. When I began looking for a job I sat at Starbucks for 2 days talking with her on Google chat about my job search and my plan of attack. She ended up sending out a tweet on twitter that one of her graduates was looking for a job in Seattle. Within 10 minutes one of her followers had a lead on a job opportunity. I quickly pitched myself on twitter to the lead. She was intrigued, asked for my resume and I got the job. (Staci, University of Oregon)

The most successful people have support systems. They realize the power of having more than one mind carve out their path to success. They also know that asking for help is not a weakness; it's a strength that shows commitment to achieving results! It really pays off to utilize the power of a support system in college. Not only will your college experience be more fruitful, but you'll benefit from this practice for the rest of your life.

A master mind is a group of two or more people who get together to support each other. A study group that meets to review concepts for a particular class is a type of master mind. Why not form a "5 Must-Know Secrets" master mind to discuss and support each other as you practice the strategies in each of your Star-sections? A master mind can be a short or long term commitment based upon the purpose of that particular group. Sometimes you'll need only one or two meetings to benefit.

A very worthwhile master mind can be formed if you approach students you admire and ask them if they'll meet you for lunch or coffee one day. Meet with them one at a time, at their convenience. When you get together with them, ask questions about how they achieve success in college. Chances are they will be flattered and pleased to talk about themselves. Learning from them will help to inspire you to find your own personal success. You don't have to spend a ton of time doing this. Just carve out the opportunity now and then.

Meet often with your advisor and come to those meetings with questions ready to discuss. Once you establish a rapport with this person, you have a coach to work with on all of the important aspects of college.

Many times I'd join a study group before an exam at someone's house - sometimes as many as 15 people. We'd quiz each other and answer each other's questions. It was a good time, and also helpful.

(Melissa, Colorado State University)

That person can help you find excellent courses, get involved on campus, find internships and research assistant positions, navigate the requirements for your major, and ensure you get everything you need to get that college degree!

When you find you connect with someone – advisor, professor, or other person whose opinion you particularly respect – you may have found a potential mentor. Working with a mentor offers you an extremely valuable opportunity to help you develop, both personally and professionally, into the person you want to be.

Don't try to figure everything out yourself!

~ #4 ~
Nourish Your Soul through Giving

Remember I told you that the deepest, level of happiness—Fulfillment Happiness – entails being a part of a greater cause? One of the best ways to benefit from this feeling of connection is to get in the habit of helping others. It's best to volunteer for no other reason but than to make a difference, rather than for recognition. The act of giving to others – as a friend, citizen, human being – is deeply gratifying and rewarding.

All colleges offer volunteer opportunities that provide awareness of life beyond campus. Make it a point to get involved in some way or look for your own less formalized opportunity to help someone in need. Whatever you choose, do it quietly, without fanfare, keeping your motivation pure. I know you don't have a lot of extra time in college, nor will you in life. Don't let this stop you from making the decision to invest some time to share your heart with others. Not only will you be a part of the solution, but you'll have discovered one of the keys to living a happier, more fulfilling life.

~ #3 ~
Treat Everyone as if They're Special

The people who feel the most fulfilled and content in their lives see the entire population around them as their extended family. They picture each person they meet as if that person wears a badge, declaring, "Please make me feel good about myself." Approaching life with this perspective sets you up with a positive energy flow that makes every day much more rewarding and pleasurable.

You can start by applying this philosophy on campus. One method I find abundantly helpful is to send out silent messages to others as I walk by them or stand in line behind them. Rather than being so lost in my thoughts that I don't notice them or being aggravated that they're taking too long in line, I send them a positive vibe, which keeps me grounded in positive energy. I silently offer these messages: "Sending you positive energy," "Wishing you abundant health," "Here is a gift of happiness," "Giving you awareness of life's simple pleasures." One message per person as I pass by keeps the energy around us positive, and I hope brings them to a better place as well.

People pick up each other's energy. Try it and you'll see what I mean. You'll not only help keep your own Soul nourished by sending these silent messages, but you'll improve the energy around you. The other person will perceive your positive aura, and you'll both benefit from it!

~ #2 ~
Have Fun!

Vital to a rejuvenated Soul is allowing yourself the luxury of time for fun! Happy people laugh regularly. The heartier the laugh, the better nourishment for your Soul. Laughter releases endorphins, combating stress and strengthening your immune system in the process. Even if you're not the one who comes up with the comedy, allow yourself to join in the laughter, to find the humor in a situation. Seek out levity. Once you get going that laughter is contagious and provides a much-needed release. Go with it and go for it…every day if possible!

There's plenty of fun to be had at college, but you may find you have to go looking for it. With each year of college, you will have more responsibilities, so at times you may need to remind yourself that fun is an important item on the "to do" list. Go to those crazy theme parties; take trips; attend midnight movies; invite new people to join you and your friends; host a spa day; go dancing; find places in town you haven't gone to before; and have parties yourself. Be a little crazy. Laugh. Dance. You'll give yourself a major boost.

And the #1 way to energize and rejuvenate…

> The best advice I have regarding college is enjoy the experience. It's a phase of your life that will be different from any other. Even if you are determined to really hunker down and study, study, study, make sure you enjoy yourself. You won't be able to recreate the experience when it's over. Try to leave college without having to say, "I regret."
>
> (Ciri, University of Texas at Austin)

~ #1 ~
Cultivate Friendships

With all that you're navigating at college, you will find there are times when you feel out of sorts and your confidence level drops a bit. Having some close friends will help you feel connected. When you spend time with them you'll feel more grounded and benefit from the oxytocin and endorphin boosts that come from having some great chats and sharing laughs. Make it a priority to cultivate and maintain friendships. They provide medicine for the Soul and are paramount to your happiness. Different friends will fulfill different needs in you and you in them. You may find some fill you with laughter; some feel like soul mates with whom you can share your deepest thoughts; others have this or that similar interest with you. And the list goes on.

Keep in mind you'll have more friends at some times in your life than others. You may find you have a huge circle in college or you may end up with just a few close friends. Sometimes you need to trust that now is not the time to have lots of friends. The number isn't important. What matters most is that you find some friends you really like.

My relationship with my roommates taught me that friendship is something that should be deeply valued. It should have less to do with having someone to sit with in the cafeteria or someone to enter a fraternity party with, and it should have more to do with the connection of your souls.

(Tami, Ohio Wesleyan University)

Jim Rohn, who was an author and motivational speaker, is well-known for this quote: "You become the average of the five people you associate with the most." This concept is one to keep in mind for college and your whole life. So pay attention to the types of friends you're hanging out with. The more you enjoy the benefits of this Star-section, the better a friend you'll be and the more success you'll have in finding friends that nourish your Soul. Great, fun, inspirational friends are a gift, and one you definitely deserve!

You may find great friends right away in college, ones that remain close for all four years and beyond. Many students find their circle of friends evolves with each year of college. You'll see how the experience unfolds for you. But the more you keep your own energy positive, the better your experience will be finding great friends. Keep in mind, too, the best vitamin for making friends — B1. When you're a caring, thoughtful, fun friend – those are the types of friends you deserve in return.

If you're just starting college, plan to sign up for at least one activity right away at the beginning of your freshman year. You'll be one of many new participants and will meet people immediately this way. If you've been at school for a while and wish to find new friends, it's still a good idea to join something. It gives you a common purpose with other students and really opens the door to making connections.

As your knowledge of the importance of positive energy increases, you may discover that some friendships seem more dominated by negative energy rather than a genuine flow of mutually positive energy and caring. Don't be disappointed if you discover others whom you thought were good friends give in to their N.E. and disappoint you. Keep your own energy positive and recognize their behavior for what it is.

Authentic and rewarding friendships cannot flourish when people lose themselves in negative-energy based relationships. Everyone has goodness in them, but not everyone learns to bring it out and use it to create a happy life for themselves. That's not your fault. Nor is it something you can allow to compromise your own positive college-journey.

Even as you find yourself busy with academics and other commitments, make it a point to spend time with your friends. This can become a bit more challenging as you move from first-year to second-year and beyond. So be sure to keep in touch with your friends as you navigate your busy schedule. You can simply text one another to make plans to meet for a meal. If someone asks you to get together but you can't make it, try to schedule something else with that person for a later date, so you don't lose the opportunity. Take it upon yourself to organize a social outing yourself once in a while, too.

I still talk to some of the friends I made freshman year (two of them were in my wedding party), but many of them faded away. At first this saddened me, but I now realize that things shifted for a reason.

The people whose company I sought out were the ones who supported and inspired me at different times, all of which ended up guiding me to where I am today. Each person left an impact on me and whether or not we are still close, they will always have a special place in my heart and memories.

(Nancy, Quinnipiac University)

~ Oh, Yes… And One More Soul Rejuvenator! ~
~ BONUS ~
The Romantic Relationship

Can't leave this one out! Cultivate friendships with guys, too, (or whichever gender would be your romantic interest) using the same principles. If you're grounded in positive energy, you'll attract people to you, including guys. If you're caught up in negative energy, you'll be more apt to attract the wrong guys for you. So, keep practicing the 5 Secrets and you'll have more success adding fun romance to your life at college, if that's something you desire.

The more you get used to developing genuine friendships with guys first, the more likely one of those friendships may start to become something more special. Being comfortable with guys as friends boosts your confidence when it comes to developing a meaningful romantic relationship. As I'm sure you know, some college guys are interested in just hooking up with as many girls as possible. If you're interested in something more meaningful that lasts longer than a night or two, get used to developing friendships first.

If you find there's someone you're particularly interested in, apply the 5-Secrets strategies in this book and see what happens! Set the goal to get to know that person better and forge a friendship, or more. "Plant the seed"; then move forward in faith on the path to making it happen. Watch for the signs and opportunities that arise to bring you success in your endeavor. Remember, you can "plant seeds" for any aspect of your college life. Have fun with it!

The best advice I received about dating in college was if you see them in an 8:00 a.m. class and they look good, they will look really good once they've had a shower and brushed their teeth!

(Lacey, Auburn University)

I had friends who stayed in my group for all four years others who had different friends but were still as close as ever. I think as we got older, we felt more comfortable with our distance, but that only encouraged us to make an effort to at least get coffee or meet once every week or couple of weeks. I say having a wide variety of friends in different subjects and interests is key. It'll expand your views, introduce you to new things, and keep things new and fresh for you.

(Jessica, University of Oregon)

99

In Summary

Fourth Star-Section: SOUL

Get Ready for Success: Express Gratitude & Replenish Your Soul!

College life is a balancing act, but it's one you can absolutely master when you regularly nourish your Soul. I hope you'll try everything on the list of Top 10 Ways to Keep Your Soul Energized in College. The more you allow yourself to regularly use these strategies, the better you'll feel! You'll stay grounded in positive energy, and you'll delight in how much you can actually achieve…all the while enjoying the college journey!

Make gratitude a natural part of your college life. See your experiences through the lens of gratitude, finding something to appreciate every day. And that includes the college goal you've set for yourself. Remember to feel grateful for having achieved that goal as if it has already happened! Applying the principles in this Star-section will keep you uplifted and energized in college, not to mention ready to receive the positive results that are coming your way!

So, let's GET THOSE POSITIVE RESULTS: In the 5th section of your Star, we'll take the final step to make your college goal…a reality!

Reflections on Soul

(Another BONUS Soul Rejuvenator: RestorativeTea!)

"TEATIPS for your college journey..."

Major strides and choices can definitely be challenging as you segue from high school to college and beyond. But when tea is added to your regimen, it can help with those challenges... and enrich your life. I wish I had known this when I was a much younger woman – what a diverse companion tea would become in my life. I have learned that nurturing your Soul on a regular ongoing basis is one of the essential keys to peace and serenity. For me tea and herbal tea add a restorative dimension to the Soul. So, I'd like to share a few of my acquired tea tips for your college journey.

Tea is a great way to meet your daily hydration needs. Fresh-brewed is best for obtaining the antioxidant-rich benefits for vitality, health and wellness. Specialty teas a/k/a loose-leaf gourmet teas are gaining in popularity and are a good value at pennies per cup. A larger selection of teas at grocery stores is regularly increasing as well. Taking the time to brew tea alone or with friends can be a way to decompress – slow down and unwind the mind while it steeps.

5 Top Herbal Teas

(Whether you prefer caffeine or not, there are tea options just for you!)

1. **Chamomile** – Good for relaxation.

2. **Peppermint** – Touted for settling upset tummies.

3. **Rooibos** – Antioxidant rich and caffeine free. Good tea alternative if caffeine sensitive.

4. **Hibiscus** – Ruby red in color, rich in Vitamin C and minerals. Delicious iced or hot.

5. **Yerba Mate** – Note – Has caffeine and is reputed to aid in energy and mental concentration.

5 Top Tea TIPS

1. **Green Tea** – Brew in water with the steam rising, NOT boiling water. Brew for 1-3 minutes. Over-steeping makes the tea bitter.

2. **Matcha** – Powdered green tea is worth investigating. It's an antioxidant heavyweight. Add lemon for even more health benefits.

3. **One of the key ingredients of tea** – L-theanine, helps to mitigate the effects of caffeine.

4. **Black Tea** – Good for heart-health. Assam and Darjeeling are popular choices.

5. **Pu-erh Tea** – Known in China as an aid in hangovers and as a digestive.

5 Soul-Enrichment Tea Rituals

1. Include pairing tea with your morning or afternoon ritual of exercise, e.g. tai chi, yoga, Pilates, walking, running, etc. to aid in energy enhancement, centering and stress reduction.

2. Add tea to combat the mid-afternoon energy slump. Take a few minutes to Energize your Soul by Mindfully Breathing for a few minutes and slowly sip a Chai (spice tea) or Herbal Chai, which is even energizing without caffeine — or your favorite tea. Pair with a snack to press on for the remainder of the day.

3. Take time for a 'Just for Me – Tea Break with Chocolate' (especially dark chocolate) yum!! Instant Soul stirring mood lifter!

4. Brew a relaxing cup of herbal tea and sip while relaxing in a well-deserved pampering bubble bath. Add a few drops of lavender or chamomile essential oils for an added spa touch. Ahhh!

5. End the day with a night-time 'Attitude of Gratitude Tea' – Mentally and physically unwind before retiring by sipping herbal tea and giving thanks for the blessings of the day. And prepare yourself for sound Soul-enriched slumber.

Gretchen Iler, CTS – Tea Sommelier
www.TeaSafari.com

"We even invented the sport of 'wall walking'..."

Sometimes it's not until after the fact that you realize what a profound experience you've had. To this day, reflecting on my freshman year in college reminds me of the importance of nurturing the soul – my own and others' – through friendship.

While I was writing Drink to the Lasses, a memoir of my experiences at a women's college, the dominant mental image for me—and that of my actual photo album—was of being in the hallway of my freshman dorm. We had a perfectly nice lounge downstairs, but we never used it. We used the hallway.

The building in which we lived used to be a convent, and the cramped size of the single rooms and the narrow passageways reflected it—we even invented the sport of "wall walking" in which we'd balance ourselves with our feet on one wall and our palms opposite, then see who could hang the highest and the longest.

The hall gave us more space and more of each other. Pizza boxes and breadstick trays were slapped on the brown nubby carpet as we passed around the contents. We lay full on our stomachs with our chins propped in our fists, memorizing Spanish vocabulary and reading Plato. In our rooms beyond, the doors hung open, ready for more reaching out, more volume for the phone, more caffeine from the little fridges.

We studied out there. Traded stories about classes. Made Christmas ornaments. Waited for the phone to ring. Told one another not to wait for the phone to ring. Took pictures of our dance dates. Once the power went out after a thunderstorm during finals week and the emergency lights above provided the only means of study. If news was announced in the hallway, it travelled from one room to the next infinitely faster than if we'd started dialing phone numbers.

In my sophomore year, I moved to a posh historic dorm with wood floors, enormous ceilings, and wide windowpanes. The hallways were enormous. Nobody sat in them. I missed my little single with the tiny passageways. Because for the entire first year, I didn't nourish my soul in college—I nourished it in a hallway.

Mary Beth Ellis
Freelance writer
Author, Drink to the Lasses
www.blondechampagne.com

"We filled the void in ourselves through 15-minute meditations…"

During the summer before starting college, my thoughts were stuck in an anxiety-filled circle of "what ifs." I was an honor student in high school and had been successful at everything. But, college was different. What if I'm homesick? What if I get bad grades? What if I don't get along with my roommate? What if I gain weight? If you are thinking the same things, you are perfectly normal.

And, I did get homesick. I did get a few grades I did not want. I got along with my first roommate. However, she was anorexic one week and bulimic the next. Her boyfriend frequently spent the night in our room and they were not shy about being "friends with benefits." And, as a result of regular midnight runs for nachos, I gained the "Freshman 15" by Christmas.

One December morning it was like my clothes had all shrunk one size. My jeans would not snap. I lay down on the floor and sucked in a deep breath, but nothing I tried made the snap close. Never had I been so disgusted with myself. The inner voice that never shuts up was all over me now. "Ugly!" "Fatso!" "Slob!" "Do something!"

I had to get the weight off immediately. I tried the cereal diet. Seven pounds came off. But as soon as I ate other foods ten pounds came on. On the grapefruit diet, ten pounds came off, but then fifteen pounds came on. I yo-yoed on and off of various crazy diets for 18 months. By the end of my sophomore year I weighed 40-pounds more than the day I started college! Well-meaning friends and family advised me that I would be so much happier if I would lose weight. Really? Did they read that on the cover of DUH? Did they not recognize my efforts?

A fresh start was what I needed, some place where no one knew me. So, that summer I transferred from a 2,000 student university to a 25,000 student university half way across the country. Self-esteem was a distant memory. That critical inner voice commanded 90-percent of my attention and energy, leaving not much for creativity, learning, or relationships. And yet, despite the extra weight, a sorority invited me to join them and a nice-looking boy asked me out.

The combination of low self-esteem and needing external validation to feel good were a recipe for dating disaster. I became whatever was pleasing to my boyfriend with no thought of myself. Let's just say that an internal conflict between values and a desire to be loved ensued.

Fast-forward to a Saturday morning in November. I was alone in the basement of my sorority house working physics problems and doing laundry – my own and my boyfriend's. When my boyfriend came to retrieve his clean clothes, he proceeded to tell me that I had done the laundry incorrectly. The collars on his polo shirts were curly. I needed to pull the shirts out of the dryer while they were still a bit damp and hang them on hangers. And, his clothes were wrinkled, which they would not have been if I had "flounced" them as I put them in the dryer, and then removed them exactly when the dryer stopped.

Whoa. Are you kidding? No "thank you"? Was I that desperate? How did I get here? Despite the plethora of humiliating moments with that guy, the laundry incident was my wake-up call. I could not make my boyfriend happy and nothing he did would fill the void inside of me. I handed him his clean laundry and broke up with him.

The following Monday I went to the health center and enrolled in their weight-loss class. The weekly class was a little bit about food choices and a lot about mindset. We learned to manage our thoughts, trading up for better feeling thoughts one believable thought at a time. We filled the void in ourselves through 15-minute meditations, connecting with the source of infinite love and energy. Each week, my self-esteem and confidence grew. I celebrated the weekly one to two-pounds of progress toward the goal of weighing 115-pounds again. Most importantly, the detour was over, and I was back on the highway of life. With no looking back I focused attention on graduating, the future, and the woman I wanted to be.

Julie Rahm
Founder, America's Mindset Mechanic
Author, Military Kids Speak
Certified Frame of Mind Coach, Inspirational Speaker
Radio Host – The Mindset Mechanic, Eastern North Carolina
Writer, The Sun Journal and The Pamlico News (weekly columns)
AmericasMindsetMechanic.com and MilitaryKidsSpeak.com

"I made it a point to be thankful and to mean it…"

I left for college a few months after turning 17, and wish I'd known then what I know now. Lauren is right: when you believe you will achieve, when you express gratitude, and when you nourish your Soul – you invite positive results.

During a 25-year career serving this great nation as a U.S. Naval intelligence officer – many times as the first female in the positions I had – I learned some valuable life lessons. Now, in my second career as an author, I'm reflecting on those lessons, and hopefully passing along some advice for readers to consider.

As one of the first female officers assigned onboard Navy aircraft carriers, I admit I was not prepared for what came. I felt overwhelmed, professionally unprepared, and overall inadequate in an extremely challenging setting. Thankful that I had been chosen for this duty, because in those days it was a real honor to be one of the few selected, I knew I had to succeed. I studied and learned more about my job every day, but I also knew I had to stay positive and feel good about something I KNEW I could do. But with so little time off work, and living on an aircraft carrier out at sea, what could I do?

I realized I could express my gratitude to sailors on the ship, whether I knew them or not. I could say something positive – thank them for what they were doing or had done – for anything as simple as cleaning a passageway. The reaction was immediate – theirs as well as my own. I recognized my appreciation for their efforts may have been the only kind words those young men and women heard that day. I made it a point to be thankful, and to mean it, and that simple behavior allowed me to know that I was doing at least ONE thing right. And the bonus: others felt better, too.

In my second career as a writer, I never thought "IF I finish this book or if I get published." I always believed it would happen. I stayed positive and never gave up when facing obstacles in my new field. When reading naysayers' advice about the hundreds of rejections I'd receive, I took note, but chose to focus my energies elsewhere. I focused on my writing and my message and in BELIEVING that my work would prove itself. I finished the book, I found a publisher, and my debut novel was selected by one of Maryland's state senators for Read Across America Day, the nation's largest reading event.

I've been very fortunate in life to have had wonderful mentors in all shapes, sizes, and flavors. People too often think of mentors only as people who can help them get ahead; this is wrong. Mentors are people who can help guide you, who may be able to provide comic relief when needed, whose life you may want to emulate in one aspect, but not in all. My mentors have been bosses, co-workers, classmates, family, friends, and even people I don't know but admire from afar. Oftentimes when faced with difficult decisions, I ask myself: "What would {this mentor} do?" Even if not able to physically speak or write to that person, I know their philosophies. With mentors in life, a person is never alone.

I wish you heartfelt success in your college journey. I leave you with some thoughts that I hope will help keep your Soul nourished and positively energized:

> **B** elieve in yourself!

> **E** xamine your interests; re-examine them regularly.

> **L** ive life today, but plan your studies ahead.

> **I** nspire others with your positivity.

> **E** xercise — something — anything — you DO have the time.

> **V** olunteer to help those less fortunate; you will learn your best lessons.

> **E** xhale, inhale, and exhale — you CAN do it.

Valerie Ormond
Captain, U.S. Navy (Retired)
Author, Believing In Horses
www.BelievingInHorses.com

Fifth Star-Section: Body

Secret 5

Nurture your Body,
for it's the vessel that carries you on your journey to success;
positive action is your driving force.

Section Five:

Mind
Instinct   Soul
Brilliance
Strength   Body

**"You must go after your wish.
As soon as you start to pursue a dream,
your life wakes up and everything has meaning."**

Barbara Sher

Your Magic Wand is almost fully-lit. You may have already started waving it at this point. The first four Star-sections – Strength, Instinct, Mind, and Soul – have set you up to achieve success. Follow the strategies in those sections, and you are on-track to getting what you want in college! Once everything else is in place, though, there's still one more step to take before you fully illuminate that Magic Wand and make it work for you. It's time to… take action! The Fifth Star-section – BODY – physically propels you along that path to reaching your goal.

Be Kind to Your Body, So You Can...Take Action!

You've already taken action the moment you head to college! You travel to campus for the first time, full of hope and expectation. You could just say, "No, on second thought I think I'll stay home where I'm comfortable and secure." But, of course, you don't because you've set the goal to attend college, and you want it badly enough to push through any anxiety and just get yourself there. So you go anyway despite nervousness. That's a huge step!

It also happens to be the way to take action with anything you're determined to make happen in your life! You push through any uncertainty about whether you will succeed, and just do it anyway. If you choose only to stay in a place of security and comfort, you'll never discover what you're truly capable of achieving! Nor will you gain the confidence that comes from looking back and realizing what you've accomplished. But it requires action to gain that confidence and perspective.

Action = Growth

That "seed" you've planted has been cared for and nourished. Now it's ready to grow and flourish!

Every time you respond to an opportunity by taking action, you grow closer to achieving your goal.

Going to college is a huge step, but it's just the beginning. The way to shine in college is to continue to set goals once you're there. We've started this process with the college goal you set for yourself in the Instinct section. Each time you go through the steps to reach a goal – as you're doing with this first goal you've just set – you'll become more inspired by what you're capable of achieving. And you'll gain the confidence to take even bigger leaps!

But no goal is ever fully realized without this final step — taking positive action to make it happen! So look for signs and opportunities that come your way, and then act on them.

When Ethlyn, a college freshman, attended her new-student orientation, she noted the advice from a dean. He mentioned that students could seek out internship opportunities through the school. Ethlyn immediately set to work making contacts at Career Services and with professors.

By the spring of her freshman year she had an ideal internship in place for the summer. When her peers asked her how she had landed such a great gig, she explained that the opportunities were there for all students to take advantage of. The counselors who helped her said it was rare for freshmen to come in for information at all! Because Ethlyn took action, she accomplished her goal.

Be prepared to respond to signs that arise for you, as well. What have you got to lose? You never know how opportunities will help you in the long run until you act on them! Try to push yourself to take action even if you're a bit

My advice is to take as many risks in college as possible. Not dangerous ones, of course, but when a opportunity comes your way – Take it.
(Amy, Webster University & Regent's College, London)

daunted by a potential opportunity. The way to overcome any fear is to do the thing you fear. Draw upon all the Secrets to help you take action anyway. You'll soon see that taking a leap doesn't require the absence of fear, it requires taking action despite any anxiety you feel. Sure there's a chance you may be disappointed with the results, but then you learn and you re-evaluate, which brings you closer to success. As Thomas Edison said, "I have not failed. I've just found 10,000 ways that won't work."

For example, if one of your goals is to make a great group of friends at school, give yourself the chance to get to know plenty of people. Stop by to say "hello" when you see an open dorm room door. Hang out in the dorm commons room. Strike up conversations with people as you leave class. Sign up for activities. Go to parties. If you make one new friend from doing all five of the suggestions above, then that's one more friend. You're on your way. The more you get used to putting yourself out there, the easier it will get!

If your goal is to over-achieve on a particular project you're working on this term, take immediate steps to make that happen. Go in to meet with your professor to clarify the parameters and to determine opportunities to amplify an aspect of assignment. Decide what you're most interested in learning about as a result of your endeavor. Then immediately begin researching that aspect of the project. Explore in the library, online, and through primary sources. Experts have become much more accessible thanks to social media, blogs, and other online opportunities. Find other students who excel in this subject and seek their input, as well. Keep all the information you glean in one place. Refer to it often, and build upon it daily. All of these steps will keep you moving towards your goal of over-achieving (and learning even more as a result).

The key is to keep your pursuits ambitious, rather than succumbing to doubts and playing it safe. Know that your core gifts make you unique and that they will lead you to success…as long as you take action! Don't let fear stop you. Instead get used to pushing through it. The more you do, the more your Magic Wand will emerge and become the driving force on your journey to success in college. Continue to evaluate your goals through the lens of the Second and Third Levels of Happiness – Glowin' and Fulfillment – and trust your Instinct. Then muster up the confidence to take action so that you can achieve the goals you set!

You can take specific steps to help keep yourself in a proactive mode in college. That way you'll be ready to act! You'll be poised to respond to meaningful opportunities with effective action when they arise! Try the following strategies to keep you motivated and on track to achieve the college goal you've set while reading this book… as well as each goal you set hereafter.

I was fortunate enough to begin working professionally as a designer while still in college. While I certainly wasn't charging a lot or taking on very many clients, I was actively promoting myself and trying to get work.

Why was I successful at this and many of my classmates were not? Confidence. I stopped treating myself like a "college student seeking starter design work" and started treating myself like a "young professional up-to-date on current design practices seeking design work." Big difference. If you treat yourself like a student, you'll be treated like one. And likewise, if you treat yourself like a professional, you'll be treated like one.
(Cole, Marshall University & University of Cincinnati)

KEEP MOVING (Towards Success) Action Steps

1) Daily Habits – Strive to have a sense of accomplishment at the end of each day. Make your bed every morning. Clear your e-mail inbox by the end of each evening. They're small accomplishments, but they keep you in a productive mindset.

2) Classes – Don't skip them. If you do, you'll feel guilty and get behind. Maintaining the habit of going to each class will help you develop a pattern of working efficiently. Professors include what they consider the most important material for you to know in their lectures, i.e., the information that will be on the tests. Also, going to class gives you the opportunity to connect with the professor and with the subject matter by asking questions. It makes a huge difference in your degree of success…and ultimately your degree.

3) Extra-Curriculars – The happiest, most successful students are also the most involved college students. Participate in at least one extra-

curricular activity each semester. Don't overbook yourself; choose one or two and be responsible to your commitments.

4) Major Department – Respond to opportunities to participate in your major department's activities. Go to the lectures and get-togethers. Speak to at least one professor each time you attend. The professors in your major department will be writing your recommendations some day. They'll also choose some students to participate in research opportunities. They may have connections to help you find internships and jobs during and after college.

Many students miss the boat on these opportunities because it feels "safer and more comfortable" not to get involved with their major departments. Don't be one of those students. Remember you're looking for signs that arise along your path to success. Don't overlook these obvious ones.

5) Research Assistant – The ideal college job is some sort of paid research assistant. Again, getting involved with your major department will help you find these opportunities. Ask your professors. Speak with assistants, administrators and TAs within the department. Research assistants get paid to help out in many capacities with projects and can lead to higher level involvement with future research. Not only will you make some extra cash in these positions, but you'll gain a different type of knowledge about your major subject, develop closer relationships with your professors, and garner experience to include on your resume.

6) Advice – One of the best opportunities you have at your disposal is to get advice. You have the benefit as a college student of not approaching someone for a job but for advice about a particular career. Set up meetings. Speak to lecturers who come to your school. The more information you gather, the clearer you will get about how to achieve your goals. Take advantage of any networking opportunities that arise. It's never too early to start this process.

7) Other Employment – Another excellent way to make some money at college is to land a campus job as opposed to working in a store, restaurant or bar. For one thing, university jobs tend to be more flexible when you need time off for school responsibilities. Also some jobs actually turn out to be study opportunities. Working in the library or

in the office of one of the college departments, for example, gives you coveted desk time during which you can study when things are slow. Don't delay. Inquire early about these jobs, as they go quickly.

8) Summer – Make the most of your summer vacations. Summer offers a break from academics and an opportunity to nourish your Soul. It's also an excellent time to look for more signs to move you along on your path to achieving your goals. Summer internships are the obvious example, paid or unpaid. They allow you to gain real-world experience, so you can uncover more information about what types of work you are drawn to as well as to cross some options off the list of choices. Summer also offers time for you to make appointments with people in careers that might interest you. Remember you're not asking them for a job, just for some advice. People are often flattered to be asked and happy to talk about themselves.

9) Study Abroad – You have a remarkable opportunity at your fingertips while you're at college! Studying abroad offers a learning experience beyond anything you can garner on campus. If there's any way you can take advantage of this life-changing addition to your college education, definitely do so!

These Action Steps will help keep you in proactive mode in college. Remember, action is what ultimately takes you to your goal! If you falter, it helps to remind yourself to enjoy the journey. If your goal inspires you, then you should have fun along the way! Even when the going gets tough at college, you can take pleasure in the knowledge that you know the steps to take to get what you want. Sure you may have some required classes you don't love. You may not always enjoy studying. In fact, it may totally stress you out at times. But the more you practice incorporating the 5 Must-Know Secrets, the more easily you'll navigate these challenges.

Keep your eye on the prize and be willing to act when opportunities arise. Once everything else is in place, it's your Body that will

When I was in college, I was determined to study abroad somewhere. It was a risk, but I was excited for the new challenge. While it was definitely daunting to travel across the world alone and attend a strange school, make new friends and find a new place to live, if I hadn't done it, I wouldn't be the person I am today. Getting out of your comfort zone isn't easy for many in college, but pushing yourself to try new things, especially ones you may never have the opportunity to do again, is worth all the risk.

(Melissa, Colorado State University)

physically take you on the final step to reaching your goal by taking action. And in so doing, it helps to honor it as an important part of the process of attaining your goals.

Your Body, Your Friend

Without the fifth Star-section – your physical being – you are all energy and no matter, so it's vital that you not ignore your Body and its needs. After all, this is the "vessel" that takes you on your path to success. You need it in order to take action!

I've already suggested that the best vitamin for making friends is B1. Well, try this same vitamin with your own Body. Be kind and communicative with it; love and respect it, just as you would any good friend. Avoid getting angry at it or treating it harshly. After all, it carries your Magic Wand, and it takes you where you need to go. Your Body is your friend.

In a way our bodies are analogous to our friends in the canine world. (If you've ever had a dog you'll especially understand this comparison.) "Max" just wants to be our friend. He wants to play with us, keep us company, cheer us up when we're down, protect us, and walk with us. When we get mad at or ignore him, Max waits until we come around and then… he's ready to play again, no questions asked. If we didn't take care of him, he'd be in trouble. He'd become hungry, sick. All he wants to do is please us, but we have to do our part and be there for him because if we don't look after him, no one else will.

I definitely gained a little weight my first year. The food was not low-fat, low-carb, which is what I eat. You probably think about your weight now, so you just need to be cognizant of the same thing in college. It feels like you're on a vacation at first, but it's a reality. So start good eating habits early on (which is still possible from cafeteria food), and you should be fine. (Laura, Chapman University)

Your Body is just as loyal to you and wants to carry you where you need to go. It's quite resilient but relies upon you to do your part. The more in touch you are with this friend, the more you benefit from its wisdom. Your Body knows what's best for you; if you listen, it will communicate with you. Start loving your Body as it does you. Treat it as the friend it is, and your Body will keep you energetic and productive.

Your Body's Fuel

Of course, respecting your "friend" entails feeding it well. It needs nutrients in order to do its part. Your Body is quite resilient, but at least be aware that processed foods, fatty foods, refined carbohydrates and sugars are not exactly "high-test fuel." Your Body will tolerate some poor choices, but it's worth better treatment most of the time. The good news is that the foods to limit are the ones that cause you to crave them the more you eat them. So, if you do cut back, you'll notice that you crave them less! You're going to have those pizza nights, late-night taco runs, junk-food driven study sessions, and more. Simply keep the word "balance" in the back of your mind. And while you're at it, remember the word "friend," too. Assess along the way: "Am I being a good friend to my Body? Do I need to re-balance my intake a bit?"

If you want attention while you're out at night, then smile and enjoy yourself people will naturally be attracted to you energy. Don't drink yourself to needine thereby forcing other people to take ca of you for the entire night. It's attentic of course, but it's the wrong kind. And whatever comfort it may give you will be short-lived.
(Carly, Binghamton University)

The same idea applies when it comes to alcohol. You're being much kinder to your Body if you at least moderate your consumption. Drinking plenty of water (especially if you're having alcohol) and eating healthy food will keep you and your Body much happier. You'll feel healthier and energized, more like yourself. Don't let your reliable "friend" down too often; you and your Body deserve better.

Down Time and Zzzzzz's

In college you find plenty of reasons to stay up until the wee hours, and if your classes don't start too early, you may still get 7 or 8 hours of sleep when you stay up late. An interesting fact, however, that your Body knows – but you may not – is that one hour of sleep before midnight is as rejuvenating as two hours after midnight. Your Body benefits more when you get to sleep by 11 o'clock (and even earlier sometimes, if you can pull it off). If you find you're often tired, you may want to adjust your sleeping habits to take advantage of the benefits of going to sleep earlier once in a while. Allow yourself to rest, so your Body can do its best for you!

A great way to make the most of the sleep you do get is to relax for 15 – 30 minutes before you go to bed. Rather than studying until you drop (because, after all, there is always more work to be done), close down for the night with at least 20 minutes to spare. Then relax with friends, play a game, watch something light on TV, chat on the computer, write in your journal, or do some other restful activity. Once you get into bed, do some Mindful Breathing (see Appendix A in the back of this book). It will relax you and can also alleviate anxiety, low-grade depression, and chronic fatigue. You'll sleep much better and wake up refreshed and ready for another productive day if you get into this habit.

Be prepared to wake up fo the 8 a.m. class but don't worry about being tired. You'll be able to take a nap in the middle of the day. (Ciri, University of Texas a Austin)

Movin' and Shakin'

Exercise is like a magic pill. Your Body loves it when you regularly get yourself moving. Exercise releases endorphins, dopamine, and serotonin that boost your mood like an anti-depressant. It keeps your Body toned, your heart-rate stable, and your immune system strong. Staying in shape through moderate exercise will help you when "sick season" approaches at college, too.

> EXERCISE. In addition to helping balance out the unhealthy eating that inevitably occurs during college, it is also a tremendous stress reducer and a great way to bond with friends. You don't need to get crazy if exercise isn't your thing; even a quiet walk on a nice afternoon can do wonders for your mood.
>
> (Becky, Hollins University)

You'll be keeping your good "friend" happier, so it can do a better job maintaining your health. Your Body's metabolism rises in response to regular exercise as well, which helps you avoid unwanted weight-gain as an added bonus.

If you're not sure what to do, try different sports. Colleges offer plenty of intramural choices. Ultimate Frisbee is a favorite that is well worth trying at least once. Swimming, biking, hiking, running, and walking are all excellent choices. If you've never tried lifting weights, you might want to get to the gym and do it. You don't need to lift heavy ones; in fact, I strongly urge you not to, as you can damage your muscles and back without realizing it if you take on weights that are too heavy. Start with 5 pounds and work up to 8 or 12 tops. You don't

> I discovered working out when I first started as an undergraduate and was going through a stressful time. It was my saving grace. I started going to the gym every morning and got so into it that I got my personal training license and started training my friends. It was time that was all about me. I could crank up the music and sweat out all my frustrations. (Amy, Webster University & Regent's College, London)

need anything heavier. Just a few biceps and triceps lifts can make a difference and keep you toned. Very important: Have someone who is trained to do so show you how to safely use weights. You'll benefit from this knowledge for the rest of your life.

Feeling Under the Weather

Chances are at some point while you're at college, you're going to come down with something. First term of freshman year is a notorious sick season unfortunately. If you do get sick at school, you can always visit the health center for diagnosis and treatment. The staff is usually extremely helpful and will lend a hand, no questions asked. Be sure you know where the health center is ahead of time, so you can find it when and if you need it.

Bottom Line

If you see your Body as the friend it is, you'll end up healthier and happier. There will always be a bulge here or a freckle there that doesn't delight you. But your Body is still the reliable friend that carries you on your journey to success! And it's going to take you right down the path to achieve that goal you've set!

> You can have the time of your life in college. Have fun. Stay up late, make memories, be crazy with your friends, always dress up for Halloween, flirt shamelessly, sing karaoke at least once, dance like a maniac, let your hair down, and remember that everyone has a few regrets when they leave college. Just make sure that it is something you'll be able to laugh at later. (Jessica, Wichita State University)

Your Body's Five Senses

Another aspect of your physical Body comes into play in this Star-section, specifically where your own happiness is concerned. The First Level of Happiness – Surface Happiness – tends to appeal to your five senses. And you'll find a great deal of that type of happiness at college. That's a highlight of the college adventure, after all!

It's also helpful, though, to realize that sensory-pleasures fall more into the entertainment category than that of long-term fulfillment. And as we know, the deeper Levels of Happiness – Glowin' and Fulfillment Happiness – are what bring long-term, sustainable joy. When we follow our senses, we seek immediate gratification. So just be aware of the limitations of the senses. That way you won't miss opportunities that offer deeper happiness, the kinds that inspire and transform your life.

> Some people see college as one big party the same way I saw it before I reevaluated my life and made some major changes. Sure, college is about fun and finding yourself, but there is plenty of time for that on the weekend. And if you spend your weekdays getting assignments complete and making sure you are prepared for class, the "self" that you "find" will probably be someone that you are happier with, anyway. (Chrissy, Drexel University)

What can keep people from living a life in which they are deeply happy and fulfilled is when they live in response to their sensory-pleasures at the exclusion of allowing the deeper Levels of Happiness to enter their lives. It can seem easier just to navigate from one type of sensory pleasure to the next without contemplating the bigger picture. It's really all about balance. Enjoy the fun of "Surface Happiness" at college, but it's absolutely crucial to also be aware that – in order to feel whole, complete, content – you can cultivate the Second and Third Levels of Happiness, as well.

You can do this by remembering all Five Star-sections as you proceed through college. You'll still enjoy all the sensory type of fun. In fact you'll enjoy it even more because you'll also be tuned into the deeper Happiness Levels. And that is knowledge that allows you to shine in college and for the rest of your life!

In Summary

Fifth Section of your Star: BODY
Nurture your Body & Take Action!

No goal is ever fully realized without taking positive action to make it happen! So push through any uncertainty about whether you'll succeed, and just do it anyway. Without taking action, you'll never discover what you're truly capable of achieving!

The Fifth Star-section– your Body – is what physically propels you along the path to success. Keep your eye on your goal and be willing to ACT when signs and opportunities arise. You can keep yourself in proactive mode by practicing the action steps in this section. They'll keep you motivated and on track to achieve each college goal you set. As you do so, respect the role your physical Body plays in taking you to success. Be kind to your Body just as you would any good friend. Respect it, love it, and communicate with it.

Enjoy the fun of "Surface Happiness" at college, but avoid indulging in sensory-pleasures at the expense of the deeper Levels of Happiness. Remember the 5 Secrets in college, and you'll enjoy all 3 Levels of Happiness that much more.

So there you have it: you now know the final step to take in order to make that goal you've set HAPPEN FOR YOU! As long as you ACT on opportunities that arise – and follow the other four Star-sections' guidelines – you're going to reach that goal… along with all the others you'll set as you move forward in your college career. You are a unique woman; your success awaits you.

Reflections on Body

"They are the voices that caution us when we should be taking action..."

When I was in college, I had this picture of the kind of person I was. It was based upon what I had done in high school, who my parents expected me to be, and how my friends saw me. It was hard to break out of that shell because I worried about what everyone would think of me if I did. Applying for a summer internship meant putting myself out there – instead of getting a job at the mall like the rest of my friends. But I just couldn't make myself do it. I did not ACT! I found it easier to fall back on old high school patterns rather than trying something new.

I didn't realize that learning to take action, to seek out the things that I wanted, was another part of the maturing process. I wish I had known that who I was in high school wasn't who I had to be in college. Our lives were much more interconnected in high school. In college, there is more freedom to learn who you want to be. I wish I had spent more time seeking the advice of professionals – learning more about career choices that would have utilized my natural talents better.

We have so many preconceived notions about who we are. We have this mental picture of ourselves developed over time by what we've done and haven't done. This image is created by our family, culture, socioeconomic class, teachers, and friends. These notions of who we think we are supposed to be and how we are supposed to act hold us back. They cloud our ability to really reach for our dreams; they are the voices that caution us when we should be taking action.

College is a time to really spread your wings, to discover the real person that lies within you, and to be bold and courageous in your pursuits. As I went through college, I eventually did become more confident and comfortable with who I was. Then I was able to start taking action.

Life is about growing. You never stop pursuing your dreams. Twenty years after graduating from college, I went back to school and changed careers. Now I'm a financial planner helping others achieve their dreams! What began in college is still going today!

Don't let anyone, even you, stand in your way.

Suparna Tirukonda, CFP®, CCPS
CERTIFIED FINANCIAL PLANNER™ Practitioner
Certified College Planning Specialist
Financial Benefits, Inc.
www.finben.com

"I regret not acting upon my interest to study abroad…"

One of my biggest regrets in life occurred when I was in college. I regret not acting upon my interest to study abroad earlier than I did. I waited until fall semester of my senior year to inquire about a study abroad opportunity in Australia, a place I had longed to go since I was a little girl. By then, however, it was too late for me to do so based on my classification and credits.

I eventually ended up spending a month in Australia when I turned thirty, but I also spent twice as much money on that one-month trip than it would have cost me as a student for an entire semester. Your college years are the time to explore the world and to do so in a very affordable way (usually for the same price as a semester's tuition which you're already paying, plus your flight – and yes, financial aid does typically apply to a semester abroad).

Once out of college and grad school, I worked for ten years as a college career adviser. I spent a lot of time encouraging my students not to make the same mistake I did and, instead, to take advantage of study abroad opportunities early on for two reasons: one, because it will give you an edge over other job candidates when employers see it on your resume, but two and most importantly, it will make you into a better and stronger person. You will learn how to step out of your comfort zone; you'll develop a better appreciation and acceptance of other cultures; you'll become less materialistic, more mature, and you may even come back a better cook than when you left!

Leaving the comfort of your home country to spend an entire semester in an unknown culture where you may or may not know the language can be scary and does require the confidence to take action. But it's the confidence you return home with that prepares you for so many things in life, things you just can't gain by staying in a bubble.

Lori Bumgarner
www.paNASHstyle.com.
Image Consultant for recording artists
College Speaker

"I started sleeping through ENTIRE classes..."

I wasn't so kind to my body when I went to college. I ate whatever I wanted in the cafeteria, and gained 30 lbs my freshmen and sophomore year. I also didn't exercise because I made the excuse to myself that I was getting it by walking to all my classes! I would go to bed at 1-2 in the morning. To make up for the lack of sleep, I started drinking coffee every morning, and whenever I needed an extra boost. But eventually it didn't work anymore.

All my lifestyle habits started to take a toll on my body. I was always tired, and I started to fall asleep in every one of my classes. I knew things had to change when I started sleeping through ENTIRE classes. Of course, that started a snowball effect because I had to make up for the lost material explained in class by studying extra late at night. I started to miss campus events because I was just too tired to make the effort. I had hit rock bottom. I thought to myself, "How am I going to survive the real world if I can't even get it together in college?"

I had had my share of abusing my body at college, and started to take baby steps to change my ways. I started making healthier choices in the cafeteria, staying away from the cordon bleus and going after healthy salads full of colorful vegetables, chickpeas, and fruits, especially grapefruit and apples. And it worked. I was taking off the famous Freshman 15! I started to rely less on coffee. Instead, I'd listen to my body and take power naps throughout the day to give it rest when it needed it. I made an effort to take extra walks, not just while going to class. I felt better about myself, and started to attend more campus events. When I heard that a career fair was going on, even though I was only a junior and not a senior ready to graduate, I took a risk that I would not have taken if I did not have the energy and decided to attend. I even went to the career development center to polish my resume. Because I was finally nourishing my body, my energy and enthusiasm shined through at the career fair, and I secured myself an internship with a local company. And because I got my foot in the door, I lined-up a job even before I graduated! I can't help thinking if I had not started to make changes and help myself, I would have missed a perfect opportunity that changed my life.

As I went to pursue graduate school to help others with what I learned during college, I realized that it was more important than ever to keep up the healthy habits. I always made an effort to get to bed before midnight. I made sure that I had a protein-rich breakfast to prevent the slumps throughout the day, and took the time to chew my food for better absorption. I started to include nuts as snacks for healthy fats to support my brain function. I tried to target half my weight in ounces of water to keep myself hydrated. If I had not taken the time to nourish my body, I would never have been able to complete both a master and doctorate program in 4 ½ years.

Now with a busy practice, I make sure I take walks every day to get fresh air, do aerobic exercise three times a week, strength training two times a week, and tai chi every morning. I'm being even kinder to my body now than I did in college, because I know I can't take care of other people without taking care of myself.

I wish I had known about all these good lifestyle habits in college, so I would have been able to take more action. I would have had the energy, vitality, and awareness to benefit from all the opportunities that were available to me. As I move forward with exciting opportunities every day, I hope you take these good lifestyle habits to heart and prepare yourself to take action!

Dr. Ann Lee, ND, L.Ac
Naturopathic Doctor, Licensed Acupuncturist
Health For Life Clinic
www.DoctorNaturalMedicine.com

If you live in the dorms you will get sick. It is just a fact of on-campus living. I found that even though classes and work will be demanding, if you don't take time to slow down when you are sick, it will take longer to get better. So the old adage of get plenty of fluids and rest still rings true in college.
(Megan, Seattle University)

Time to... Shine!

"You are what you repeatedly do.

Excellence is not an event – it's a habit."

Aristotle

So, what do you think? Did you grasp the gist of the 5 Must-Know Secrets? I hope you get a sense now of the power you have available to you, the power to take charge of your college success and happiness. I know we've just covered quite a bit of information. It's a lot to take in and synthesize at first.

But now you're primed to use the Action Guide in Part II, where you'll be able to practice and build upon your understanding of the 5 Secrets. All the Action Steps you've just finished reading as part of your overview, you'll now have the opportunity to practice. The questions I've been asking, you'll be able to contemplate and respond to. The strategies I've been sharing, you'll apply and track. Simply take it a step at a time – very quickly you'll see how easy it is. It's also exciting because as you implement the activities in the Action Guide, you'll notice some remarkable changes in your life at college. Your Magic Wand will begin to ignite – one STAR section at a time – and as it does, you'll feel your stress level decrease and your confidence increase.

That's when the process will start to speed up automatically. You'll be energized by what you're accomplishing and before long, you'll realize you've become an orchestra conductor – and the symphony is called, "Your College Life." You'll be proactively orchestrating your success in every facet of your life. And you'll realize how easy it all is. In fact, it will become second nature.

All of this happens as you power up each STAR section on your Magic Wand: Strength, Instinct, Mind, Soul, and Body. You ignite them and then you get them fired up to full brilliance. The more you practice the strategies in each section, the brighter your STAR becomes… and the more you pave the way to your own success.

That's why we started by having you choose one college goal to get you going. Once you move through all five STAR sections to implement that goal, you'll get a sense of the power of your Magic Wand. Then you can keep using the same strategies to accomplish another goal, then another, until using the power of your Magic Wand becomes a way of life for you… and makes you shine in every facet of your college life!

You'll open a door that will allow you to step – even leap – through it to a newly-found place of inspiration and clarity of purpose. You'll experience first-hand that no challenge is insurmountable. It's not that you'll no longer face obstacles; they'll remain a fact of life. It's your reaction to them that will change. You'll find that the daily challenges of college-life will no longer test your confidence in your own ability to succeed. You'll even start to see those challenges as opportunities in disguise!

The closer any of us gets to success when we move towards achieving a goal, the more obstacles we'll face. But if we don't know this fact, then those obstacles will stop us in our tracks. When you're aware that obstacles are actually a sign that you're going to reach your goal, you become empowered to push through them and succeed! That's a major difference between achievers and non-achievers. Non-achievers become daunted by the obstacles and retreat. Achievers expect obstacles and see them as a sign of soon-to-be-realized success.

I encourage you to refer to the 5 Must-Know Secrets regularly to keep you moving towards getting what you want. Incorporating the 5 Secrets takes practice. Even when they become more natural to you, you'll still have to remind yourself of them when those obstacles arise.

My Own TEST of the 5 Must-Know Secrets

Obviously, one of my goals was to share with you the powerful Secrets in this book. I faced many obstacles along the way to making this book a reality, so I had to keep the STAR sections on my own Magic Wand illuminated in order to push through those challenges when they arose. I could give you many examples, but here's just one little taste.

One morning I headed to the library – computer and notes in tow – thrilled to have an entire day set aside for writing. I couldn't wait to get started. I arrived at 10am sharp, the opening time indicated on the library's website, only to be greeted by a "CLOSED" sign. I was completely taken aback. I work much better in a quiet library than in my distraction-filled Manhattan apartment. Not to mention, finding the time for writing at all is always an undertaking with my schedule. So I set off again, determined to find an alternative place to write. Three bus trips, two technology glitches, and one pulled muscle later, I finally sat in a library, having lost two hours of coveted work time.

I couldn't believe it. Such stress just to get to this starting point! I felt discouraged by the lengths I had been forced to take that morning, and I was tired and sore. I found myself questioning why this had to be so hard and thought maybe I should just call it a day. My heart sank as my motivation slowly seeped out of me. (See how negative energy can snowball?)

As I stared at my computer screen in frustrated contemplation, it finally dawned on me. I closed my eyes and said to myself, "That's N.E. NOT me!" That changed my perspective, and I reevaluated the morning's challenging events. I remembered that the closer we get to accomplishing something important in our lives, the more obstacles we'll have to overcome. The hurdles I had jumped over for two hours were actually signs that I would, in fact, achieve my intended goal. I really had to stop to remember this fact rather than let my negative energy take the control it wanted!

I immediately shifted my focus to feeling grateful for the fact that I was sitting in a quiet library with plenty of time left to write all afternoon! I also found the humor in the situation by realizing that I had gone through a sort of TEST. As often happens to me, I faced a situation that required me to test the 5 Must-Know Secrets. And once again, they worked. They always do! That realization allowed me to shift my energy to the positive place it needed to be. I took a couple of deep breaths and enjoyed the moment (Momentous Living). Finally, I was ready – and excited – to work. I was smiling when I placed my fingers on the keyboard and started to write.

But then – at that very instant – a deafening alarm rang out in the library. I jumped! It hit me like a punch in the gut. I looked around to figure out what was happening, holding my hands over my ears for what seemed like an eternity. Finally, the alarm abruptly stopped. It was eerie; everyone was completely silent. I think we were all stunned. A few moments later, a voice chimed over the loud speaker to inform us that "This has been a test, only a test. Pardon the interruption, but these tests are very important." We all stared blankly at each other, and then it hit me. I actually began to laugh at loud. What had I just realized a moment ago…that my morning of obstacles had been a TEST? Talk about a confirmation! Yes, yes – a test. Well, I guess I passed. What followed for me was a productive and rewarding day of writing!

College = Ideal Time

It helps tremendously to remember that life's opportunities require dodging temporary defeats and seeing them as signs of your assured success. Every time you face a challenge, ask yourself, "How can I use this as fuel to help me move forward towards my goal?" The answer will come as if by magic (or maybe even over a loud speaker!). And when that happens, you'll have this incredible, eye-opening realization. It's a feeling that so many students – and I – find utterly empowering. It feels as if you've just waved… your own Magic Wand.

RIGHT NOW while you're in college is the best time to learn the power at your disposal. All you have to do is start incorporating the 5 Must-Know Secrets as part of your college life, and the rest will take care of itself. When you navigate your journey with this sense of purpose, you will be rewarded every step of the way.

The 5 Must-Know Secrets

1) **Discover and explore your unique core gifts. Their Strength is the foundation for your success.**

2) **Follow your Instinct to recognize the goals and dreams that are right for you. There you'll find the confidence so vital to your success.**

3) **As you envision yourself achieving your goals, use the power of your Mind to keep negative energy from sabotaging your success.**

4) **Get ready to catch the success that's coming your way through Gratitude and Soul-rejuvenation.**

5) **Nurture your Body, for it's the vessel that carries you on your journey to success; positive action is your driving force.**

I'm honored to have shared the 5 Secrets that have already changed the lives of countless college girls. Follow them and you'll regularly experience the inspiration that comes from reaching goal after goal in college…and for the rest of your life. When you're inspired, you will inspire others, and that is the greatest gift you can give the world. Move on to the 5 Must-Know Secrets Action Guide to give them a try – you'll see what I mean!

Part II

The 5 Must-Know Secrets

Action Guide

The 5 Must-Know Secrets

Action Guide

Now that you have an understanding of the 5 Must-Know Secrets, it's time to give them a try!

The following pages will help you practice incorporating the strategies from each Star-section. Here you can track your progress as you move towards the short-term college goal you set. You'll also have the opportunity to record your responses to Action Step questions and monitor your success with the strategies presented in Part One.

One of the best ways to ensure that you'll achieve a goal is to write down your intentions. The Action Guide will get you in the habit of doing exactly that!

Take a deep breath – exhale – and get ready to SHINE by proactively adding the 5 Must-Know Secrets to your college life!

5 Must-Know Secrets
Action Guide

Secret 1

Discover and explore your unique core gifts. Their Strength is the foundation for your success.

Strength in Action!

Discover Your Core Gifts

As you now know you'll be on your way to loving college, and the rest of your life, when you begin to uncover your own core gifts! It's actually an exciting process. It doesn't happen over night, but it's fun – and eye-opening – once you get the hang of it. So why not begin right now? You'll be amazed by what you learn about yourself! Here's how to get started.

First, Look Within Yourself

1: A) What activities did you enjoy as a child, and what did you particularly like about them?

....

....

....

....

....

....

B) When you were younger, what did you think you wanted to be when you grew up?

....

....

....

....

....

....

C) What themes emerge for you when you think back on your younger years in this way?

....

....

....

....

....

....

2: A) Begin to tune into what is joyful work for you, what gives you the greatest pleasure. (Usually it will be what causes you to lose all sense of time as you are engaged in it. Notice when you are naturally focused and not easily distracted.) Keep a list here of activities you discover at college that fit this description:

....

....

....

....

....

B) What were you doing the last time you felt inspired in this way?

....

....

....

....

....

....

3: If you could be doing anything in five years, what would it be?

....

....

....

....

....

....

4: Make a list of your natural abilities as you become aware of them. You won't yet know how it will all fit together in your future. That's okay. Keeping track of what inspires you will help you tremendously as you navigate your college years.

....

....

....

....

....

....

....

Second, Look To Others

You'll find it enlightening to ask people who know you to weigh in on this topic. Although it may seem strange at first to ask others questions about yourself, doing so will really inform the process. Remember, your most powerful gifts are often ones that you aren't even aware you possess! You'll be surprised what people may realize about you that you haven't yet realized yourself.

Ask Them to Answer These Questions:

1) What do you think I do naturally well?

2) What 5 words come to mind when you think of me?

3) What would you call upon me to help you with?

You can record their answers here:

Person One _____ **(name)**

1) What I do naturally well

....

....

....

....

....

....

2) The 5 words that come to mind about me

....

....

....

....

3) He/she would call upon me to help with...

....

....

....

....

....

....

Person Two _____ **(name)**

1) What I do naturally well

....

....

....

....

....

....

2) The 5 words that come to mind about me

....

....

....

....

....

3) He/she would call upon me to help with...

....

....

....

....

....

....

Person Three _____ **(name)**

1) What I do naturally well

....

....

....

....

....

....

2) The 5 words that come to mind about me

　　　　..

　　　　..

　　　　..

　　　　..

　　　　..

3) He/she would call upon me to help with…

....

....

....

....

....

....

(Feel free to ask more than three people! You can record their responses on another sheet of paper or on your computer.)

Now, Consider Both Perspectives

Look for common themes between your own personal assessment responses and the ones you receive from other people. Keep in mind that your core gifts may seem so natural to you that you've never stopped to consider them gifts at all. They are! And uncovering them will help you tremendously as you proceed with your college experience.

Some common themes (between your responses and other people's)…

....

....

....

....

....

....

Now based upon those common themes, write down what you think your core gifts might be. (This is a list you'll want to add to as you learn more about yourself.)

My Core Gifts

....

....

....

....

....

Skills You Acquire Along the Way

A skill is a bit different from a core gift. It's an ability that comes from learning and practicing something. When you combine your core gifts with skills you acquire, that's when you really have something special to offer the world. So – in addition to your core gifts list – keep a list of skills you acquire in college. And as you do, bear in mind that the skills you bring to the job market will fall into three categories: Physical, Mental, and Interpersonal. All are helpful for doing a job well.

My Skills List

1) **Your physical skills (motor related talents that you do with your hands or body)**

....

....

2) **Your mental skills (cerebral abilities that come from your mind)**

....

....

3) **Your interpersonal skills (social talents that cultivate personal relationships)**

....

....

(You'll be very glad to have these lists when you're working on your resume!)

Two Especially Important Skills:

Time Management and Connecting with Others

Remember I mentioned the importance of these two skills in particular? Time Management is a "mental skill" and Getting Along with Others is an "interpersonal skill." They'll help you excel in any career; they're also vital for enjoying success in college. If you know you need some practice in these areas, use the following checklists to help you. (Then add them to your "My Skills List" above.)

Skill #1

Time Management

When it comes to managing your time, it helps to look at the academic part of college as your "job" at the moment. Plan ahead of time when you're going to "take care of business," and you'll be amazed at how many hours you'll have left for FUN!

Proactive Time Management – Check List

❑ **Schedule your free time.** Rather than the other way around, actually decide when you're going to relax, have fun, etc. Then school work is what you will do the rest of the time.

How did this work for you? How might you improve?

....

....

....

❑ **Keep up the momentum between classes.** Rather than stopping and starting all day long, when you have a short block of time available, you can review notes, read a short article, run errands, or e-mail a professor. Make your days productive. You'll get much more done, and you'll stay alert and motivated.

How did this work for you? How might you improve?

....

....

....

❑ **Learn how to be a smart studier.** You'll be inundated at times with reading assignments, and frankly, you won't be able to read every word. Check out chapter and section headings first to get an overview of the topics. Then skim certain parts while reading some sections more thoroughly. You'll get a sense of what works best for each class as you go along.

How did this work for you? How might you improve?

....

....

....

❑ **Take advantage of meal time.** "Breaking bread" with your friends is fun and a great way to beat stress, but you don't have to eat every meal together. You might want to get used to eating one meal by yourself each day. Have it in the dining hall or bring it outside, to your room or some other quiet place. Bring some reading with you or notes to review and use the time to accomplish something. Then you can really appreciate your social meal times when you have them.

How did this work for you? How might you improve?

....

....

....

❑ **Speaking of your room, don't study there.** You'll get much more accomplished in the library. That will leave you more time for socializing, relaxation, and other fun activities. It can take students their entire freshman year to figure out that they accomplish much more when they go to the library to study. You can get a head start by getting into this habit right away. Better to save your dorm environment for fun time.

How did this work for you? How might you improve?

....

....

....

❑ **Make your own deadlines.** You have much more freedom with your schedule in college, which means you have much more responsibility to figure out when you're going to get assignments done. Although a project may be due in two weeks, you'll need to add more deadlines to that time-frame, your own deadlines. Otherwise two weeks becomes this ambiguous, extended, unproductive period and before you know it, you've come to the point where you're one day away from the due date with nothing yet accomplished.

How did this work for you? How might you improve?

....

....

....

❑ **Plan backwards.** No matter what the assignment, work backwards from the due date and make some headway on it every step of the way. If you have a test in three weeks, create chunks of study time well in advance, so you're working towards the test date in preparation. Don't plan to study for the test for the entire day before it takes place. Try to avoid doing anything in its entirety right before it's due.

How did this work for you? How might you improve?

....

....

....

Skill #2

Connecting with Others

Being in the unique position you're in – pretty much starting from scratch with college friendships – offers you a valuable opportunity. That is, it's a chance to sharpen your interpersonal skills, something you'll find hugely beneficial to your career success as well as for building a circle of friends now.

 Forging Positive Connections – Check List

❑ **Face the Person** – Your body positioning is an important factor in making a dialogue exchange positive. Turn towards the other person and lean ever-so-slightly in her direction. Avoid crossing your arms in front of your chest.

With whom have you tried this lately?

....

....

Comments

....

....

❑ **Make Eye Contact** – What color are your roommate's eyes? How about the students' across the hall? Your professors'? Make it your goal to find out! Always look into someone's eyes upon meeting him. In fact, try to be the first to establish eye contact.

With whom have you tried this lately?

....

....

Comments

....

....

❑ **Enjoy the Interaction –** Whatever words you use, let people know you're happy to meet them through the upbeat sound of your voice. Feel happy to meet new people and you will sound welcoming.

With whom have you tried this lately?

....

....

Comments

....

....

❑ **Use Names –** Make the effort after you learn a person's name to use it! That way the new name will pass from your short-term to your long-term memory. Whenever possible, envision a person you know or someone famous who has the same name as the person you're meeting. Then think of something they have visually in common. If you allow that visualization to enter your mind, you will have a much easier time remembering the new person's name the next time you meet her.

With whom have you tried this lately?

....

....

Comments

....

....

❑ **Remember Your Goal –** Connecting with people you meet doesn't mean you're inviting them to come to your home for summer vacation. You're just getting acquainted. Avoid making judgments, just engage. It's not a competition; it's an interaction. Smile!

With whom have you tried this lately?

....

....

Comments

....

....

❑ **Show Interest** – Being interested is actually more important than being interesting. The fact is most people love to talk about themselves. Use this information in your favor. Use it to remind yourself not to go on and on about you! (Yes, really!) And let others talk about their favorite topic: themselves! So, ask open-ended questions. Then respond by showing you're listening and encourage them to tell you more.

With whom have you tried this lately?

....

....

Comments

....

....

❑ **Be Upbeat** – See these connections as positive opportunities. Even if you're having a challenging day, make your goal be a positive spin. This strategy results in a win/win: you get a reprieve from thinking about the day's challenges, and the other person gets to talk about herself.

With whom have you tried this lately?

....

....

Comments

....

❑ **Pick up on Cues** – While you're actively listening, notice the other person's conversational style. The most obvious qualities are volume, speed, and degree of animation or energy. As you pick up on these cues, subtly alter your own patterns to harmonize with the person to whom you are talking. For example, if your new acquaintance speaks rather softly, tone your own volume down as well.

With whom have you tried this lately?

....

....

Comments

....

❑ **Keep your Cool** – Ask other people questions and be tolerant of differing opinions. You'll rarely persuade others to change their opinions anyway, so enjoy the art of a good discussion while respecting another's point of view. You'll feel much more empowered at the end of a conversation if you make it a practice to respect the people with whom you are conversing and keep your sense of humor.

With whom have you tried this lately?

....

....

Comments

....

Recognize the opportunity you have at your fingertips to excel in time-management and making positive connections. Be patient with yourself along the way because you're simply not going to get it right every time. But now's the ideal time to practice!

Remember ~ The more you allow yourself to be an explorer, the more information you'll have to help you keep track of your unique STRENGTH. So survey the terrain, make note of what you discover, and you'll be that much closer to falling in love... with the rest of your life!

5 Must-Know Secrets
Action Guide

Secret **2**

Follow your Instinct to recognize the goals and dreams that are right for you. There you'll find the confidence so vital to your success.

Instinct in Action!

Dare to Dream

Think about your own life for a moment. If you could have your ideal life, what might it look like? Really let yourself visualize the possibilities. Don't worry about the "how" right now. We'll get to that. Simply savor the images that come to your mind when you allow yourself to imagine your idea of a dream life.

What might it look like? Allow yourself to visualize the possibilities. Jot down the ideas that come to your mind:

....

....

....

Ultimately, when you envision a "dream life," you're coming up with ideas of what you think will make you happy. So, to achieve the "life of your dreams," you're really striving for personal, long-term happiness.

The Three Levels of Happiness

In order for your dreams to result in genuine happiness that will be yours for your lifetime, they should deliver all three Levels of Happiness, "Surface Happiness," "Glowin' Happiness," and "Fulfillment Happiness."

To become more acquainted with each category, begin right now to think of what activities you've experienced over the years that appeal to each level of happiness.

1) Surface happiness (immediate gratification happiness)
(Activities you've experienced that appeal to this 1st level)

....

....

2) Glowin' Happiness (when you are in the flow of doing something you love)
(Activities you've experienced that appeal to this 2nd level)

....

....

....

3) Fulfillment Happiness (comes from being a part of a cause that is bigger than yourself)
(Activities you've experienced that appeal to this 3rd level)

....

....

....

Set a Short-Term Goal

As you continue to figure out your long-term vision for your life, you can actually get yourself on the path to making it happen before the fact. Simply choose a short-term college goal RIGHT NOW, one that is meaningful to you. Then practice using the 5 Secrets to take you through the process of making that goal a reality. Once you achieve just one goal in this way, you'll already have a sense of what I've been describing – that empowering feeling of having made it happen... as if you've waved a Magic Wand. Then the more you continue with additional goals, the better you'll get at "making magic happen" to achieve your desires!

The first step to achieving a goal should always be to write it down. You have a far better chance of making it happen when you start out this way. So, take the time to choose a goal right now in any category — academic, extra-curricular, social – whatever inspires you! Something you'll feel great about accomplishing.

My Goal

....

....

....

....

Happiness Levels Test

Whenever you set a goal, you'll definitely want to put it through the Happiness Levels Test. If you don't analyze your goal through this lens, then the 5 Secrets won't necessarily be able to "work their magic" to help you achieve it. This is especially true when it comes to overruling your negative energy. If you can't connect your goal to at least two, preferably all three, levels of happiness, then you may not be able to take advantage of the power of your mind to make it happen. You'll see this for yourself through trial and error, but going through the Happiness Levels Test is what sets you up for success. It really is crucial.

Here's how to do it: Give that goal you've just written down a little more thought by answering the following questions:

1) Why is this goal important to me?

....

....

....

2) How will I feel once I achieve it?

....

....

....

Now analyze your responses through the lens of all three levels of happiness.

How will this short-term goal appeal to my...
1) Surface Happiness?

....

....

....

2) Glowin'Happiness?

....

....

....

3) Fulfillment Happiness?

....

....

....

If you haven't been able to connect the achievement of your goal to at least two out of the three happiness-levels, give the questions a little more thought. If you absolutely can't connect it to more than one type of happiness, you should revise it or choose a different goal.

Remember – The more your goal excites you, the more passionately you'll desire it. And the more passionately you desire it, the more clearly you'll see the path to make it happen as it emerges for you.

Now acknowledge your goal with confidence

You won't know at this point exactly how you're going to make it happen; simply allow yourself to feel confident that you will achieve your goal! Check the box to acknowledge your confidence in "planting the seed" to get moving on this goal! Also sign your name below.

I am consciously setting my short-term college goal and have written it down. I don't know right now exactly how I will achieve it, but I am "planting the seed." I'm confident that if I follow the steps in each Star-section, I will achieve my goal.

....

(Sign Here)

☺

5 Must-Know Secrets
Action Guide

Secret **3**

As you envision yourself achieving your goals, use the power of your Mind to keep negative energy from sabotaging your success.

Mind in Action!

Discover the Power of Your Mind

Now it's time to harness the power of your Mind to help you achieve your goal!

Strategy One

Take Control of that Negative Energy (N.E.)

Remember negative energy (N.E.) is a manifestation of fear. It's natural to some degree, but it needs to be recognized and controlled when it sends out messages, such as "I can't…," "I'm not capable of…," and "I don't deserve." You can change how you think by recognizing this negative energy as left-brain security warnings gone awry – not truth. Here are the strategies to practice when your N.E. tries to "think" you out of achieving that goal you set:

    N.E. Control Check List

☐ **1) Recognize It** – Simply seeing your negative energy for what it is provides the first step to overruling it. When you find yourself thinking, "I'm not capable of achieving my goal," for whatever reason that pops into your mind, realize that your negative energy is trying to take control. See it for what it is: left-brain security warnings gone haywire (NOT the real YOU)!

What are you thinking that is making you question your capacity to achieve your goal?

❏ **2) Combat It** – ASSERT! Declare firmly – "That's N.E. not ME!" Say it out loud. State it with confidence! You'll cause the N.E. to weaken.

Write the words here to help you with this assertion

....

....

❏ **3) Back Away from It** – Create some distance between you and those sabotaging doubts, so you can view them as an object to be confronted, not a reflection of the REAL YOU. (Positive energy is the real you, not this distracting N.E.)

Describe your process of moving away, of separating yourself from your N.E. Include your acknowledgement of its being separate from your true self.

....

....

....

❏ **4) Celebrate It** – Realize that negative energy is often a sign of something good to come! So, when those discouraging thoughts enter your mind, celebrate the fact that you're getting closer to reaching your goal...and that you WILL achieve it! In fact – say "thank you" for (whatever obstacle you're facing)!

Thank you for

....

....

I know I can learn from/overcome this obstacle and that I am closer to

....

....

Some ways I might move through this obstacle are

....

❑ **5) Laugh at It** – One excellent way to free yourself from the daunting vibe of negative energy is to refuse to take it too seriously. Smile knowingly and laugh at it rather than giving into its tricks. Laughter really works; it stops negative energy it its tracks. (Remember, that's N.E. not ME!)

Write down your declaration that this obstacle is really something to laugh at— not something to make you give up on your goal.

....

....

....

❑ **6) Overrule It –** The best way to get through a challenge is to keep going! Your positive energy has already begun to take over at this point. Use it to push through whatever obstacles you face in achieving your goal.

It's not whether you're going to face obstacles on your way to reaching your goal, it's how you deal with them that makes the difference. You now know that all you have to do is move past this bump and you're back on the path to achieving your goal. Take a deep breath and prepare to move forward.

Write down your intention to push ahead.

....

....

....

You can overrule negative energy in all facets of your college life by going through these same Action Steps. And, as you do, be aware that you will make mistakes. They're an important part of your experience. So be ready to…

❑ **7) Forgive Yourself –** Mistakes are simply learning experiences to get you closer to your goals! You'll really overrule your negative energy when you take the word "failure" out of your vocabulary when it comes to reaching your goals. You'll have "successes" and "learning experiences" along the way. Remember, you're in a "No Failure Zone" when you've positively set your intention to reach a goal!

Write down one success you've had and one failure learning experience.

1) Success

....

....

2) Learning Experience

....

....

Now congratulate yourself for BOTH of them! ☺

Strategy Two

Mental Imaging

Now that you've practiced overruling your negative energy, let's focus positively on your goal. Whatever you choose to focus your attention on actually becomes your reality. Your mind has this power! So you may as well use it to your advantage to help you achieve the college goal you've set for yourself.

Try it right now: Picture yourself having already accomplished your goal. Really focus on it, making the image as clear and as desirable as you can. What does your success look like? Spend some time savoring the images that emerge for you. Now take a moment to describe the feelings that surface as you picture your own success.

When I picture myself having already achieved my goal I feel...

....

....

....

It's important to return to that picture in your mind and the feelings that vision evokes often as possible in order to get the most mileage out of this powerful strategy you have at your disposal! You'll keep your positive energy dominant this way. Take a few moments to return to that mental picture at some point each day.

Add one or both of the following tangible aids to your Mental Imaging, and you'll start cruising toward the achievement of that goal of yours.

Mental Imaging Aid: Create a Vision Journal

1) Find a journal or notebook that you like.

2) On its pages, paste photos that symbolize to you the achievement of the college goal you've set. Use magazine photos, pictures from the internet, and even your own photos. Each photo will represent an aspect of the success that will result when you achieve your goal. These photos are for you only, so it's not important that others understand what each one represents.

3) Now add quotations that inspire you and notes to yourself that will help motivate you. Include statements of gratitude for having already achieved your goal.

4) Keep adding to your Vision Journal as you come across more relevant pictures and quotations. Also continue to write motivating notes to yourself when you feel so inspired.

Describe your experience using a Vision Journal to help you achieve your goal.

....

....

....

Try to spend some time with your Vision Journal each day. Carry it with you when you can. Take a few minutes to savor the pictures, quotes and notes within it as often as possible. It will inspire you!

Second Mental Imaging Aid: Create a Vision Board

1) Get a piece of poster board or large drawing paper.

2) On it draw and/or paste pictures that symbolize to you the realization of the college goal you have set. As with the pictures in your Vision Journal, the pictures you choose for your Vision Board should be meaningful to you. It isn't necessary for your Vision Board to make sense to anyone else.

3) Put no words on your Vision Board, except your heading: (Your name's Vision Board). This is a pictures-only device.

158

4) **Hang your Vision Board in a place where you'll see it each day, perhaps on the inside of your closet door or on your bulletin board. Then take a few moments to look at each picture – and at the entire collage as a whole – at least once a day.**

Describe your experience using a Vision Board to help you achieve your goal.

....

....

....

The secret of Vision Boards is that they appeal to both sides of the brain. Since they utilize images, the right experimental side of the brain gets stimulated, excited to move forward towards achieving the goals pictured. The practical left side of the brain doesn't recognize images the way it does words, so it doesn't get all stressed out by the movement toward positive change. You get to import vital positive signals to your mind this way without unsettling the left brain.

Strategy Three

Momentous Living

Momentous Living is another effective way to use the power of your Mind. It's like a switch that you can use to instantly change how you're thinking. That switch provides a natural – and instantaneous – antidote to negative energy! When you make it a habit to turn on this switch, you'll become an expert at utilizing the power of positive energy to make good things happen for you at college. Be sure to take advantage of this game-changer to help you move closer to your goal!

Momentous Living – Check List

❑ 1) Whenever you become aware that negative energy has overtaken your thoughts, stop and ask yourself this question: "What is good about this moment in time…right now?"

❑ 2) Be aware that sometimes the answer will be more obvious than others, but there is always something positive about the present moment. It can be as simple as appreciating the warm bed you're sleeping in or the meal you're eating. It can be the "big picture" reminder that you're appreciative to be getting a college education. The more you practice looking for it, the better you'll get at finding it!

❑ 3) Start to observe yourself when you begin to buy into your negative energy. You'll notice the types of tricks you get tempted to allow the N.E. to play. Then if you STOP and focus on what's good about this moment in time, you'll be able to avoid the false, misleading thought patterns N.E. can cause, and you'll stay on track to achieving your goals.

Give it a try. Tease out an answer by writing whatever comes into your mind until you nail it:

What's good about this moment right now is…

....

....

....

Did you feel a shift in your energy? You absolutely stop negative energy in its tracks when you practice Momentous Living.

Remember – momentous means important, meaningful, outstanding. And those are words that should describe your life…and every moment in it! The path to achieving your short-term college goal – and eventually your bigger vision for your life – should be an enjoyable one.

Write your intention to enjoy traveling the path to achieving your goal.

....

....

....

Look for what is good about each moment in time, and you will find it. As you do, you'll begin to feel more happiness within yourself and with your life in general.

5 Must-Know Secrets
Action Guide

Secret **4**

Get ready to "catch" the success
that's coming your way through
Gratitude and Soul-rejuvenation.

Soul

Soul in Action!

Feel Gratitude & Replenish Your Soul!

Now that you're utilizing the Power of your Mind by holding onto a clear vision of yourself achieving your college goal, it's time to prepare to get what you want. Time to put on that softball glove and get in position to "catch" what's coming your way, namely the achievement of your goal!

So let's practice these two ways of preparing you to "receive" what you want –

First – Apply the principle of Gratitude.

Second – Energize and replenish your Soul.

Strategy One

Apply the Principle of Gratitude

The #1 strategy to prepare yourself to reach your goal is to feel grateful for having achieved it, as if it's already signed, sealed and delivered! Get yourself to the point where you can feel the pleasure of having already achieved it. Spend some time luxuriating in the joy it brings you. Once you set your goal, you must feel grateful that you will achieve it as if it has already happened. Gratitude powers up your Magic Wand!

Practice the Attitude of Gratitude

1) Each morning, start out by being grateful that you WILL absolutely achieve the college goal you've set for yourself. Look in the mirror, smile, and say "thank you" for the achievement of that goal, as if it's already happened!

Express your gratitude here for the fact that you will achieve your goal.

....

....

....

....

2) Next come up with at least one aspect of your life for which you feel grateful. What do you appreciate today? (Is it something you're looking forward to, an activity you're enjoying in your life right now, a new friend you've made, a class you like, an achievement, your health?)

Write down what you are grateful for today.

....

....

....

....

3) As you look in the mirror, get a glimpse of that Magic Wand inside of you. Focus on the STAR at the top, and notice how it's filled with brilliant light. Now see and feel that brilliant light shine right through you out into the world. Take a deep breath. Know that you're on your way to having a productive and enlightening day. Tell yourself, "I will be receptive to recognizing opportunities that come my way today, even ones that may masquerade as challenges."

Write your intention to feel gratitude for the opportunities as well as the challenges that come your way today.

....

....

....

4) As you walk to class, make it your intention to feel gratitude. Gratitude keeps you energized, and positive energy brings you positive results. You're sending it out; therefore, you're going to get it back.

Remind yourself right now that by the time you reach your destination you will feel the positive energy that comes to you as a result.

....

....

....

....

....

(Remember you should do this every day!)

Gratitude keeps you energized, and positive energy brings you positive results. Whatever goal you've set, you chose it because of the happiness you think it will bring you, so dwell on those happy feelings.

Strategy Two

Regularly Replenish your Soul
Much of college is a balancing act, a challenging one at that. At times you may feel as if you just aren't in control of navigating all that you need to do, let alone all that you want to do! This issue is crucial because when you are in control, you have the confidence you need to achieve success.

The balancing act doesn't go away. But you can maintain the ability to control it by keeping yourself positively energized. As you know, our "negative voices" thrive on spinning negative energy around in our heads. One result is that we become disappointed in ourselves, damaging our own self confidence. You can clear away this sabotaging negative energy by allowing yourself to replenish your Soul. You'll also keep yourself confidently on the path to achieving the success you seek!

To ensure you take the time, you so need and deserve, to replenish your soul – keep track of ideas you try on the following checklist.

How to Keep Your Soul Energized in College!
Top 10 – Check List

❑ 10) **Establish a Positive Environment for Yourself –**

What have you "done with the place" to help keep you uplifted?

....

....

....

❑ 9) **Create a "Dear You" File**

How many entries do you have so far?

....

Describe how it feels to read them from time-to-time.

....

....

....

❑ 8) **Find a Spot**

Where is your spot?

....

What sorts of things have you thought about lately while you were there?

....

....

....

How does it feel to "escape" from college life in this way?

....

....

....

....

❏ **7) Breath Mindfully, Listen to Guided Inspirations -** Deep breathing – also called Mindful Breathing – helps boost your body's immune system and combats stress. It also energizes your Soul. Please see Appendix A for detailed instructions on how to practice Mindful Breathing.

When did you try Mindful Breathing?

....

How did it make you feel?

....

When else might you try it?

....

The Guided Inspiration is a relaxing spoken-word recording that you can listen to at your convenience to give you motivation and encouragement. Please go to Appendix B for instructions on how to access a Guided Inspiration.

Which Guided Inspiration did you listen to?
How did it make you feel?

....

❏ **6) Write in your Journal**

What happened when you asked a question in your journal and then proceeded to answer it? Describe the experience you had.

....

....

....

❏ **5) Find Mentors, Coaches, and Master Minds**

Who might be potential coaches or mentors for you at college?

....

....

....

What sorts of master minds might you form?

....

....

Whom might you ask to join them with you?

....

....

❑ **4) Nourish your Soul through Giving**

Have you found a volunteer opportunity that you have taken advantage of in college?

Or perhaps you are being especially helpful to someone on or off campus?

❑ YES   ❑ NO

How does your involvement in this activity make you feel?

....

....

....

(Note – if it's too time consuming for your busy schedule, seek opportunities that won't take as much time.)

❑ **3) Treat Everyone as if they're Special**

Have you shared your positive energy with someone around you lately? If so briefly describe it.

....

....

....

What has been the reaction, if any, and how did it make you feel?

....

....

....

❑ 2) Have Fun!

What have you done for fun lately?

....

....

....

When is the last time you had a good laugh?

....

....

How did you feel afterward?

....

....

❑ 1) Cultivate Friendships

Are you keeping your mind open to making new friends?

❑ YES   ❑ NO

Are you remembering that it takes a while to figure out who your closest friends will turn out to be?

❑ YES   ❑ NO

What sorts of things have you done to give yourself the opportunity to meet and get to know people?

....

....

....

What else might you do?

....

....

....

Oh, Yes... And One More Soul Rejuvenator!

❑ **Bonus) The Romantic Relationship**

Are you cultivating friendships with guys, too?

☐ YES ☐ NO

Is there anyone special in whom you might have a romantic interest?

☐ YES ☐ NO

If you find there's someone you're particularly interested in, try out the strategies in this book and see what happens! Set the goal to get to know that person better and forge a friendship, or more. "Plant the seed"; then move forward in faith on the path to making it happen. Watch for the signs and opportunities that arise to bring you success in your endeavor.

Remember, you can "plant seeds" about any aspect of your college life. Have fun with it!

Come back to this Top 10 list often. Try as many of the strategies as possible! The more you keep your Soul energized, the better you'll feel! You'll keep yourself grounded in positive energy, and you'll delight in how much you can actually achieve!

5 Must-Know Secrets
Action Guide

Secret **5**

Nurture your Body, for it's the vessel that carries you on your journey to success; positive action is your driving force.

Body in Action!

Take Action!

You're well on your way to achieving your goal at this point, and now the time has come to… take action! The Fifth Star-section will physically propel you along that path to making that goal a reality.

So be prepared to respond to signs that arise for you. Have your eyes open and be ready to respond with positive action. What have you got to lose? You never know how opportunities will help you in the long run until you act on them! Try to push yourself to take action even if you're a bit daunted by a potential opportunity. All the other Secrets will help you! Sure there's a chance you may be disappointed with the results, but then you learn and you re-evaluate, which brings you closer to success.

You'll find it easier to act on opportunities that arise for you along the way if you're regularly proactive in your approach to college life.

Action Strategies

Try these specific steps to help keep you in a proactive mode in college. That way you'll be poised to respond to meaningful opportunities with effective action when they arise. And you'll be on track to reaching your goal!

Pro-Action Mode – Checklist

❑ **1) Daily Habits** – Strive to have a sense of accomplishment at the end of each day. Make your bed every morning. Clear your e-mail inbox by the end of each evening. They're small accomplishments, but they keep you in a productive mindset.

What have you tried and what seems to work for you?

....

....

❑ **2) Classes** – Don't skip them. If you do, you'll feel guilty and get behind. Maintaining the habit of going to each class will help you develop a pattern of working efficiently. Professors include what they consider the most important material for you to know in their lectures, i.e., the information that will be on the tests. Also, going to class gives you the opportunity to connect with the professor and with the subject matter by asking questions.

How are you doing with classroom attendance?

....

How is it paying off for you?

....

....

❑ **3) Extra-Curriculars** – The happiest, most successful students are also the most involved college students. Participate in at least one extra-curricular activity each semester. Don't overbook yourself; choose one or two, and be responsible to your commitments.

What extra-curricular activities have you tried to far?

....

....

What else might you like to try while you're at school?

....

....

❏ **4) Major Department** – Respond to opportunities to participate in your major department's activities. Go to the lectures and get-togethers. Speak to at least one professor each time you attend. The professors in your major department will be writing your recommendations some day. They'll also choose some students to participate in research opportunities. They may have connections to help you find internships and jobs during and after college.

Many students miss the boat on these opportunities because it's "safer and more comfortable" not to get involved with their major departments. Don't be one of those students. Remember you're looking for signs that arise along your path to success. Don't overlook these obvious ones.

What sorts of activities/opportunities does your major department offer?

....

....

....

....

Check off the ones you have participated in.

Star the activities you might still try.

❏ **5) Research Assistant** – The ideal college job is some sort of paid research assistant. Again, getting involved with your major department will help you find these opportunities. Ask your professors. Speak with assistants, administrators and TAs within the department. Research assistants get paid to help out in many capacities with projects and can lead to higher level involvement with future research. Not only will you make some extra cash in these positions, but you'll gain a different type of knowledge about your major subject, develop closer relationships with your professors, and garner experience to include on your resume.

What opportunities are there for Research Assistants in your major department?

....

....

Star the ones you have or plan to apply for.

❏ **6) Advice –** One of the best opportunities you have at your disposal is to get advice. You have the benefit as a college student of not approaching someone for a job but for advice about a particular career. Set up meetings. Speak to lecturers who come to your school. The more information you gather, the clearer you will get about how to achieve your goals. Take advantage of any networking opportunities that arise. It's never too early to start this process.

From whom have you already sought advice?

....

....

Think of others with whom you might set up a meeting.

....

....

Who are some of the speakers scheduled to come to your school this year?

....

❏ **7) Other Employment –** Another excellent way to make some money at college is to land a campus job as opposed to working in a store, restaurant or bar. For one thing, university jobs tend to be more flexible when you need time off for school responsibilities. Also some jobs actually turn out to be study opportunities. Working in the library or in the office of one of the college departments, for example, gives you coveted desk time during which you can study when things are slow. You will need to inquire early about these jobs, as they go quickly.

What job opportunities have you found?

....

....

Where else might you look?

....

....

❏ **8) Summer –** Make the most of your summer vacations. Summer offers a break from academics and an opportunity to nourish your Soul. It's also an excellent time to look for more signs to move you along on your path to achieving your goals. Summer internships are the obvious example, paid or unpaid. They allow you to gain real-world experience, so you can uncover more information about what types of work you are drawn to as well as to cross some options off the list of choices. Summer also offers time for you to make appointments with people in careers that might interest you. Remember you're not asking them for a job, just for some advice. People are often flattered to be asked and happy to talk about themselves.

What will you do next summer?

....

....

If you're not sure, where will you go to get information?

....

....

Who might be able to help you with this?

....

....

❑ **9) Study Abroad –** You have a remarkable opportunity at your fingertips while you're at college! Studying abroad offers a learning experience beyond anything you can garner on campus. If you don't take advantage of it, you're missing out on a tremendous addition to your college education.

What programs does your school offer for off-campus study?

....

....

Star the ones you might be interested in

....

If you might want to study abroad, when will you speak to your advisor about planning your courses and credits so that you can figure out how to make it happen?

....

....

The strategies on the previous checklist will keep you in proactive mode in college. Remember, action is what ultimately takes you to your goal! Even when the going gets tough at college, you can take pleasure in the knowledge that you know the steps to take to get what you want. Each time you go through the steps to reach a goal you'll become more aware of what you're capable of achieving, and you'll gain the confidence to take even bigger leaps!

Write down at least three actions you will take to move you closer to achieving the college-goal you've set for yourself while reading this book. Then check them off as you implement them, and add to the list as you move closer to your goal:

Actions I will take to achieve my goal of

....

(Write your goal here.)

❑ **#1**

....

....

....

❑ **#2**

....

....

....

❑ **#3**

....

....

....

❑ **#4**

....

....

....

❏ #5

....

....

....

❏ #6

....

....

....

❏ #7

....

....

....

❏ #8

....

....

....

❏ #9

....

....

....

❏ #10

....

....

....

Your Body, your Friend

In order to take action to achieve your goal, you need your physical Body. After all, this is the "vessel" that takes you on your path to success. You need it in order to take action! It is, therefore, vital to honor it as a crucial part of the process. Be kind and communicative with it; love and respect it. Treat it as the friend it is, and your Body will keep you energetic and productive.

Be Kind to Your Body — Check List

❑ **1) Fuel**
What healthy foods and drinks have you had in the past week?

....

....

What have you consumed lately that haven't been the kindest choices for your friend, your body?

....

....

How do these two lists compare? Simply be aware of the balance between the two when it comes to your food and drink choices.

❑ **2) Rest**

Keep track of the time you go to sleep and the time you wake up for the next week. Also pay attention to what you do for the last twenty minutes before you retire.

Day 1

....

Day 2

....

Day 3

....

Day 4

....

Day 5

....

Day 6

....

Day 7

....

How are you feeling overall? Keep the information above in mind in case you need to revise your schedule in order to stay healthy and feel more energized.

❑ **3) Exercise**

Keep track of how often you get some sort of exercise for the next week. You can fill this section out at the same time you are writing down your sleep habits.

Day 1

....

Day 2

....

Day 3

....

Day 4

....

Day 5

....

Day 6

....

Day 7

....

Aim to engage in some sort of exercise for at least ½ hour each day.

❑ **4) A Friend in Need**

What first aid supplies do you have handy?

....

....

Where is the campus Health Center?

....

....

Where is the nearest hospital or medical center off campus?

....

....

❑ **5) A Friend Indeed**

Write down at least three things you appreciate about your body.

....

....

You're on your way to achieving your goal – with much more success to come – as long as you take care of your Body and use it to take action!

Your Five Senses

Remember — the first level of happiness – Surface Happiness – tends to appeal to your five senses. And you'll find a great deal of that type of happiness at college. It's also helpful, though, to realize that sensory-pleasures fall more into the entertainment category than that of long-term fulfillment. And as we know, the deeper Levels of Happiness – Glowin' and Fulfillment Happiness – are what bring long-term, sustainable joy. When we follow our senses, we seek immediate gratification. So just be aware of the limitations of the senses. That way you won't miss opportunities that offer deeper happiness, the kinds that inspire and transform your life.

It's really all about balance. Enjoy the fun of "Surface Happiness" at college, but it's absolutely crucial to also be aware that – in order to feel whole, complete, content – you can cultivate the Second and Third Levels of Happiness, as well.

You've already written down past activities that fall into each level of happiness. Start to keep track of what activities you engage in from now on and what level(s) of happiness each one is appealing to for you. Analyzing your activities through this lens will become automatic after a while. And knowing which happiness level(s) you're satisfying helps you balance your activities. When you enjoy all three levels, you have a richer, more rewarding college experience.

1) **Surface Happiness –** immediate gratification happiness. (Eating, having fun at a party, buying something new, flirting, etc.)

Write down what you do for the next few weeks that would fall into the category of surface happiness.

....

....

....

....

2) **Glowin' Happiness –** When you're in the flow of doing something you love. (Playing music, writing, computer technology, math challenges, athletic activity, etc.)

Jot down activities you are involved in for the next few weeks that result in your being in the flow, perhaps they cause you to lose track of time.

....

....

....

....

3) **Fulfillment Happiness –** being involved with an activity that is bigger than yourself, often it benefits others either directly or indirectly. (Putting on a show of some sort, starting a business on campus, engaging in volunteer work, etc.)

Write down any activity (or activities) you find yourself engaged in this term that gives you a sense of contributing to a community with a higher purpose.

....

....

....

....

After keeping these lists for a few weeks, make an assessment. If you're heavy in some happiness levels activities but don't have anything to add to others, then you can rebalance your choices in order to feel more joyful at college!

Also take note of activities that fall into more than one category of happiness for you. Write them down here:

1) Two levels of happiness

....

....

....

....

2) All three levels of happiness

....

....

....

....

Remember all five Star-sections in college and you'll enjoy all three Levels of Happiness that much more. Getting used to this practice can help tremendously when it comes to making decisions about your future. You're destined for abundant success…as long as you take action!

In Closing

5 Must-Know Secrets Action Guide

Using this Guide will be an ongoing process. You can keep it handy and fill it in now and then whenever you have a few spare moments. As you write your responses, you'll be reinforcing the Star-section strategies. And before you know it, you'll get to the point where the 5 Secrets become a natural way of life for you. You'll enjoy a more confident stride and more clarity in your journey.

I've seen what an extraordinary difference the 5 Secrets make in the lives of students who embrace them. My sincere wish is that you, too, will enjoy a successful and joyful college experience. You are now on the path to doing exactly that.

Congratulations!

Not only are you a college student...

but now you know:

✓ how to accelerate your own college success,

✓ how to SHINE – both in and out of the classroom,

✓ the 5 Must-Know Secrets for Today's College Girl!

Appendix A

Guide to Mindful Breathing

Mindful Breathing offers a way to rejuvenate without spending money to go to a spa! It's a simple and productive way to de-stress, get grounded, and gain clarity.

1) Why practice Mindful Breathing?

Mindful Breathing is a strategy that many college students with whom I have worked find remarkably beneficial, even life-changing! It teaches you that you have – within you – all that you need to relieve your own stress.

It releases tension by giving you a break from whatever is weighing on your mind. As a result you are able to heal and nourish yourself - both mentally and physically. We are all so accustomed to multitasking and responding to the many distractions around us that we need to learn how to relax and clear our minds. Once you learn Mindful Breathing, its restorative qualities allow you to enjoy more success with whatever you need to accomplish because it gives you a clearer focus as well as a comforting sense of peacefulness.

2) What is Mindful Breathing?

It's the process of temporarily stopping those thoughts — of stopping all thinking — for a short time. In our minds we naturally talk to ourselves all the time. And when we do, we tend to dwell on whatever is worrying us to the point where it snowballs and seems much worse than it actually is. Our own thoughts mislead us and warp our sense of the reality of a situation. That includes allowing our worries to escalate to the point of causing us severe stress that sometimes manifests into physical symptoms. (For example, have you ever been so stressed that you end up with a headache, stomach ache or worse? Mindful Breathing will help you keep that from happening!)

It takes a bit of practice, but it gets easier each time you do it. And before you know it, you recognize those negative — potentially snowballing — thoughts when they come, and you are able to head them off at the pass. By freeing your thoughts of your schoolwork or whatever is looming in your mind, you get a mini-vacation from them. You create an opening that allows you to shift the moment, to regain a healthy perspective, and to breathe a sigh of much-needed relief.

3) How do you it?

Just follow these steps to Mindful Breathing:

- Sit down with your eyes closed and your feet on the floor.

- Take a deep breath, becoming aware of your body and its energy as you inhale. Then slowly exhale, releasing the tension you feel inside. And repeat. Inhale a deep, slow breath...and exhale slowly, releasing more tension. Inhale positive energy; exhale all the tension.

- Focus on individual parts of your body with each deep breath you take in. Students find that concentrating on their eyes, shoulders, hands, and feet provides a quick de-stressing experience. For example, as you slowly inhale and exhale, say to yourself,

**"In — I focus on my eyes.
Out — I release the tension from my eyes."**

You will release the tension in each of those parts of your body and allow them to rest. The quality of your breathing will immediately improve, slowing down naturally and soothing you

- Spend anywhere from two to twenty minutes engaged in Mindful Breathing, depending upon what your schedule allows.

You can practice Mindful Breathing while you walk, too. (Just be sure to keep your eyes open while you do so; you still have to watch where you're going.)

Here are the steps for Mindful Walking:

- Repeat the word "in" to yourself for each step you take during your inhale, and repeat the word "out" for each step during your exhale.

- Focus on the soles of your feet and on your breathing rather than your thoughts.

- Remember to concentrate on your steps – on the soles of your feet – as you breathe (in, in, in...out, out, out), not on your thoughts

- Allow your thoughts to leave your mind as you enjoy the freedom of this restful walking process.

People are always in such a rush to get where they are going. Mindful Walking allows you to enjoy the actual walking-process and heal yourself as you do.

The goal with both Mindful Breathing and Mindful Walking is to focus on your breathing and your body's energy exclusively, turning off your thoughts for a few moments. You'll have to catch yourself at first because your mind will naturally wander. But little by little, you'll be able to turn off your thought-process completely for a short time, which is incredibly refreshing and ultimately empowering. Once you get better at it, you'll have the power to diffuse your own stress, healing yourself both mentally and physically.

4) When should you do it?

You can do it just about any time: as a study break, when you're chilling in your room, at the computer, taking an exam, walking to class, and – especially – right before you go to sleep at night! The more you do it, the more you will realize that every time you engage in Mindful Breathing you are giving yourself a much-deserved treat. The more you do it, the more grounded and rejuvenated you will feel.

One of my students told me that she could only find time for Mindful Breathing (when she first started doing it) while she was walking to and from classes. So she practiced Mindful Walking. Simply incorporating it as she walked around campus, this student told me it made a world of difference. She reported feeling a heightened sense of clarity and confidence. After some practice, she mastered the art of Mindful Breathing and was able to use it to keep herself from becoming overly stressed.

Remember the goal is to turn off your thoughts as you engage in Mindful Breathing. Try it tonight when you are lying in bed before you fall asleep.

Appendix B

The Guided Inspiration

Guided Inspirations provide the secret weapon for maintaining that necessary balance so crucial to a rich college experience. They are relaxing spoken-word recordings you can listen to at your convenience to help you keep your life at college the joyful journey it can – and should – be.

Students tell me that when they listen to Guided Inspirations, they immediately feel more

- **Confident**
- **Motivated**
- **Refreshed**
- **Energized**

I suggest students have Guided Inspirations readily available on their computers and MP3s, so they can benefit from the positive energy these soothing recordings provide.

To download a complimentary Guided Inspiration, simply go to www.CollegeGuidanceGuru.com and click on "Free Gifts."

They are so easy to listen to any time you want the lift that comes from a renewed sense of clarity, perspective, and purpose. Enjoy!

Index

A

Academics, 15,26-27,72-73,90,98,114,174
Achievers, 49,65,125
Action
  effective, 112,171
  positive, 108,110,171-177
  proactive, 112,114,125,131
Action Steps
  core gifts, 23-24,133-140
  dare to dream in college, 46,149-150
  forging positive connections, 30-32,144-147
  gratitude, 87-88,163-164
  happiness levels test, 48,151-152
  momentous living, 75,159-160
  negative energy control, 69-70,154-156
  proactive mode, 112-114,172-175
  time management, 28-29,141-143
Advice, importance of getting, 113,174
Alcohol, 116
Anti-depressant, 116-117
Antidote to negative energy, 73,159
Apartment, 91,126

B

Baebler, Erin, 80
Balance, between positive and negative energy, 64
Balance, importance of, 90,116,118,178,180-181,187
Balancing act, college, 15,86,90,164
Body, Fifth Section of Your Star
  body defined, 109-110
  fuel for your, 115-116
  importance of b., 18,125
  taking care of your, 115-118,177-180
  your friend, 115,180
Brain
  left, 63-64,73,154
  right, 63-64,73
Bumgarner, Lori, 121
Business courses, 27

C

Career placement office, 27
Career, preparing for a, 22-24,26,30,72,9
113-114,141,144,174-175
Catch success, 84-86,127,161-162
Clark, Jennifer, 37
Classes
  attending, 24-26,112,172
  choosing, 22,25
  keeping up the momentum between, 28,1
Coaches, finding, 94-95,166-167
College success, your, 45,64,124
College, going is just the beginning, 21, 109-110
Compartments, in the life of a college girl,
Computer skills, 27
Confidence, acknowledge your dream with, 47-48
Continentino, Paige, 56
Core gifts, 20,22-24,27,43,133-140
Course syllabus, 73

D

Dare to Dream in college, 39-40,43-46,61
73,149
Dear You file, 92,165
Del Gatto, Susan, 77
Department, major, 113,173
Depression, 116
Dopamine, 117
Dorm room, 74,91-92,111
Dream
  = a seed, 47
  dream-life, 40,49
  your own (not someone else's), 44

E

Ellis, Mary Beth, 103
Employment, while in college, 113-114,17
Endorphins, 96,117
Energized, importance of staying, 17,86,1
24,164,169,187

Energy
    dance, 63,68
    internal, 60
    negative energy control, 64-75,
    154-157
Exercise, 117,179
Explorer, approach college like a, 24-27,32,147
Extra-curricular activities, 46,112-113, 150,172

F
Fatigue, chronic, 116
Fear, overcoming, 64,66,93,111,153
Females, need to replenish, 90
Find a spot, 92,165
Flower, seed to, 47-48
Food, 115-116,178
Foundation for success, 20,127,132
Friendships
    authentic and rewarding, 98
    best vitamin for making, 97,115
    cultivating, 97,168-169
    negative-energy based, 98
    starting from scratch with, 30-32,144
    with guys, 99,169
Fulfillment happiness, 41-43,48,95, 118,149-152,180-181
Fun
    having, 15,41,44,96,99,114,118,167,180
    making time for, 28-29,96,141-142,167
    scary, 63

G
Getting along with others, 27,30-32,141, 144-147
Glass half-empty mindset, 62
Glass half-full mindset, 62-63
Glowin' happiness, 41-43,48,149-152, 180-181
Goal(s)
    long term, 40,46-49,150
    setting, 45-49,73,150-152
    short-term, 46,49,61,69,150
GPA (grade point average), 25-26
Gratitude, 84, 86-89,162-164
Growth-cycle, seed to flower, 47-48, 110
Guided inspirations, 93,166,187,192

H
Happiness
    3 levels of, 41-43, 48,87,112,118, 149-152
    fulfillment, 41-43,48,95,118,149-152, 180-181
    glowin', 41-43, 48, 149-152,180-181
    inviting, 62
    levels test, surface, 48,151-152
    ultimate goal of, 40,149
Harmony, secrets work in, 18-19,86
Health center, campus, 117,180
Hill, Napoleon, 42
Huber, Joy, 52

I
Ideal life, create your, 40,45,149-150
Iler, Gretchen, 101
Instinct, Second Section of Your Star
    basic human, 59
    importance of i., 18,125
    instinct defined, 43-44
    using your, 43-44,48-49
Internships, 64,95, 110,113-114,173,175

J
Jobs, college, 113-114,174
Journal(s)
    vision, 72,158
    weight-loss vision, 87-88
    write in a, 93-94,116,166
Joyful work, 23,134

L
Lee, Dr. Ann, 122

Lewis, Tracy, 79
Life, your momentous, 74,160
Limitations of the senses, 118,180
Lottery winners, 42
Lucas, Kristen, 81

M
Magic Wand, Your
    how to access your, 16-19,39,45, 75,87,
    109,111,124-125,150,162
    star on top of, 17-18
    what it can do, 16-19,39,45,75,109,111,
    124-125,150,162
Major department, 113,173
Major, choosing a, 22-26,92
Master mind groups, 94,166-167
Mattocks, Carolyn, 34
Medders, Amanda, 54
Mental imaging, 70-73,157-159
Mentors, 94-95,166
Mind, Third Section of Your Star
    energy dance inside, 63-64
    importance of m., 18,125
    mind defined, 59-60
    power of, 59,64,66-68,70-73,151,154-159,
    162
    voice inside, 63-64
Mindful breathing, 93,166,184-186
Momentous living, 73-75,126,159-160

N
N.E., 64-70,75,98,154-160
National Honor Society, 65
Newton, Sir Isaac - Third Law of Motion, 85
Nutrition, 115-116,178

O
Obstacles, overcoming, 18,44,64,88,125,
155-156
Olson-Rogers, Michelle E., 51
Ormond, Valerie, 106

P
Positive energy, 62-66,68-69,73,75,
87-99,155-156
Possibilities, focus on, 44,49,62,70-71,
73,157
Potential, your true, 59
Principle of gratitude, 86-89,162-164
Process of elimination, 26
Purpose, sense of, 12,41,91,98,125,127,
181,187
Pursuits, ambitious, 111

R
Rahm, Julie, 104
Reflections

    on body, 120
    on instinct, 51
    on mind, 77
    on soul, 101
    on strength, 34
Research assistant, 95,113,173
Romantic relationships, 72,99,169

S
Secret weapon for college success, 16
Secrets, the 5 Must-Know
    secret #1, 20,127,132
    secret #2, 38,127,148
    secret #3, 58,127,153
    secret #4, 84,127,161
    secret #5, 108,127,170
Security and comfort, temptations of, 101
Seed analogy, 47-48, 60, 86, 110
Seitz, Becca, 36
Self, your true, 44,155
Senses, your five, 118,180-181
Serotonin, 117
Shine, both in and out of the classroom, 44,183
Sick-season, college, 117
Signs and opportunities, notice, 66,89,
99,110,113-114,127,169,173-175

Skills
  computer, 27
  interpersonal, 27-28,30,140,144
  mental, 27,140-141
  physical, 27,140
  writing, 27
Sleep
  lack of, 90
  making the most of, 116,178,186
Social scene, 15,28-29,69,90,96-98,
142,168
Soul, Fourth Section of Your Star
  energize and replenish your, 86,
  90-99,162,164-169
  importance of s., 18,125
  mates, 97
  medicine for the, 97
  soul defined, 85-86
Speaks, Avril Z., 57
Sports, 117
Spot, find a, 92, 165
Star Sections
  body, 108,171
  instinct, 38,149
  mind 58,154
  soul, 84,162
  strength, 20,133
Star, on top of your Magic Wand, 17-18
Strength, First Section of Your Star
  foundation of, 20,132
  importance of st., 18,125
  strength defined, 22
  your natural, 25
Stress
  decrease your level of, 124
  how to beat it, 16,28,63-
  64,86,93,96,124,142,166,184,187
  many students' constant
  companion, 90
  studying-induced, 114
Success
  accelerating your college, 45,183

catch, 84-86,127,161-162
get ready for, 84-86,127,161
orchestrating your own,
40,60,64,72,125
system for, 12
your happiness and, 15-16,64,75
Summer break, 114,174
Surface happiness, 41-43,48,118-119,
149-152,180-181
Switch, a magic, 73,159
Syllabus, course,73

T
Tangible aids for Mental Imaging, 72-73
Test(s)
  doing poorly on a, 26,71
  happiness levels , 48,151-152
  of the 5 Must-Know Secrets, 125-127
  preparing for, 29,112,143,172
  vocational, 26-27
Think and Grow Rich - Napoleon Hill, 42
Think, change how you, 60-61, 65, 73,
154, 159
Third Law of Motion - Sir Isaac
Newton, 85
Time management, 15, 27-28, 140
Tirukonda, Suparna, 120
Top 10 ways to keep your soul energized
  in college, 91-97,165-169
Tortorici, Julie, 82

U
Unique, what makes you, 22,25,32,
42,111,119,127,147

V
Vision boards, 72,158-159
Vision journals, 72,158
Vitamin, best one for making friends,
97,115
Vocational tests, 26-27
Volunteer work, 95,167,181

W
Want versus plan, 71
Weight-gain, 16, 87-88, 117
Writing skills, 27

About the Author

Lauren Salamone is an award-winning mentor to college students. For 15 years she has made it her mission to help students "have it all" –

- **to excel in college,**

- **to enjoy the fun, so crucial to the experience,**

- **to use college to create their ideal lives.**

Through her presentations, workshops, Guided Inspirations, books, newsletters, and mentoring services – Lauren shares simple and powerful strategies that have fostered success in young women from high school seniors to college and graduate students – and many of their moms along the way. She inspires students to do, to be, and to have all they desire in college…and for the rest of their lives.

Lauren brings a unique perspective to her work with college students. Her years as a high school English teacher gave her valuable insight into empowering and connecting with today's youth. Drawing upon her advertising and marketing experience – at corporations such as CBS, Inc. and Westinghouse Broadcasting – she enlightens students on the importance of setting and reaching goals, as well as discovering what it takes to succeed. Her training began at St. Lawrence University, where she earned her B.A. with honors. She went on to earn her M.A. at New York University where she was the Graduate Valedictorian.

To learn more about Lauren's presentations, workshops, and services, visit **www.CollegeGuidanceGuru.com.**